SOAPY SMITH UNCROWNED KING OF SKAGWAY

BY

Howard Clifford

Soapy Smith
Uncrowned King of Skagway

ISBN 0-911803-09-2

Cover photo courtesy of Joseph J. Smith. Other photos as indicated. Many thanks to Jefferson Randolph Smith's grandsons, the late Joseph J. and Randy Smith. Also his great grandson Jeff Smith and the Jeff Smith Collection, the Trail of '98 Museum in Skagway and scores of others in providing material and information without which this book could not have been written.

Sourdough Enterprise
16401 3rd Ave. SW
Seattle, WA 98166

Printed in the United States of America

CONTENTS

Jefferson Randolph (Soapy) Smith as he appeared at the time of his visit with his cousin, Edwin "Bobo" Smith of the Washington (D.C.) Post. He hobnobbed with politicians, charmed the news media such as W.F. Hayes of the New York World, internationally renowned Richard Harding Davis and others. He also secured an government concession permit to build and operate a hotel and other facilities at St. Michael at the mouth of the Yukon River. - Clifford Collection.

PROLOGUE

Of all the famous figures in the Old West, Jefferson Randolph "Soapy" Smith stands out alone as a maze of inexplicable contradictions. He was a paradox, as many-sided as he was incomprehensible.

He became the Master of the sure thing game, the Prince of confidence men, Emperor of the Denver underworld, Ruler of Creede and uncrowned King of Skagway.

Many state that it was a shame that Mark Twain's days as a wanderer in the West ended without his making the acquaintance of Soapy Smith.

It would have taken such as Twain to explain Soapy and his methods of separating suckers from their money and his curious yearning to be acclaimed a patriot and public benefactor by his fellow citizens.

He was of the generation that grew up on the success stories of Horatio Alger — anything was OK if no physical harm was done. He became a sort of folklore hero before he met a violent death at the peak of his colorful career.

In some ways he was years ahead of his time. Although operating on a small stage the tactics he used — the hard and disciplined core of ruthless men working undercover — the presenting of himself as a champion of the people — the careful cultivation of the basic elements of the community, business, labor, church and press — were the marks of later day European dictators.

He lived on the Western Frontier where no odium was attached to being a gambler or saloon keeper. Gambling was legal and a bartender was one of the most respected persons in the community — generally better thought of than doctors or lawyers.

Jefferson Randolph Smith was the first of the West's bona-fide gangsters - perhaps its most successful. Compared to his modern day successors he presented an angelic mien. Smith was both a brigand and a philanthropist, a Robin Hood to the sentimental, a black scoundrel to others and a puzzle to all.

He was as dexterous with a pistol as he was at wrapping a bar of soap, shuffling walnut shells and an illusive pea or dealing a deck of cards, but preferred to rely on the nimbleness of his mind and the smoothness of his tongue.

He hobnobbed with presidents, his articulate speech left politicians mesmerized, he swayed unruly mobs with his oratory and fleeced the gullible with his gentle, soft spoken southern accent. He was the most artful grifter to frequent the mining camps of the West.

A kind and generous family man, he was a loyal friend in his personal relationships and took pride in viewing himself as a public

"I AM THE UNCROWNED KING"

TITLE WHICH THE DEAD "SOAPY" SMITH GAVE HIMSELF.

He Looked More Like a Rancher Than the King of the "Grafters" —His Immense Fortune Lost at Gambling Table or Spent for Fun.

The Post-Intelligencer presents this morning the last picture of "Soapy" Smith, the "uncrowned king of Skagway," who was shot and killed by Frank Reid, July 8, on a wharf at Skagway, while attempting to break up a citizens' indignation meeting.

Smith has assumed a typical pose and it does not require any effort of the imagination on the part of anyone who knew him to recall how "Soapy" would stand in front of a bar with gold spread out in front of him, inviting the crowd up to drink. No matter how much money he had in sight, he remained there until it had been wiped out in drink or the crowd left him.

From Smith's appearance no one would be led to suppose that he was the king of Alaska grafters and that he controlled them as surely and methodically as a general his army. He was 5 feet 6 inches tall and weighed 144 pounds. He was slouchy in appearance and made no pretensions to dress. He wore a very stubborn, full black beard. His chest was covered with a thick mat of black hair. He had dark, expressive eyes, and his features when closely inspected gave one the impression that he knew a thing or two.

It is estimated that "Soapy" made $1,500,000 through grafting in twenty or twenty-five years and that during that time he spent more money than any other grafter or big-spending sporting man. There is no question that he lost more money gambling during his exciting career than any other man in the United States. He would cover a faro layout or roulette table with ... and it did not make much dif-

"'SOAPY' SMITH.
(From his last photograph.)

He came originally from Sweet Home, Or., where his family is well known. In 18__ Reid had trouble over domestic affairs with James Simon. It was claimed that Simon

The Seattle Post Intelligencer called attention to the fact that it was Soapy Smith himself who concocted the sobriquet "Uncrowned King" of Skagway." The story, along with a picture of Soapy taken shortly before his demise, appeared eight days after his death. - Clifford Collection

benefactor. He was an impostor unparalleled, master of every "con", ruler of rogues and vagabonds, friend of the friendless, protector of criminals, builder of churches, and benefactor of the godly and needy.

The term "sure-thing game" with its companion phrase "sure thing man" came into the language as a result of his remarks addressing the Clergical Association of Denver at the Peoples Tabernacle. He preached an inspirational sermon against drinking, citing himself as a bad example although he did not drink to excess. He was a student of Baptist ministry and a pillar of the church. He donated turkeys by the hundreds to the needy at Thanksgiving and handed out $20 bills to the homeless at Christmas. Many prominent Denver business leaders willingly turned large sums of money over to Smith at Christmas to be added to his own generous donations to the needy.

He spent thousands of his own funds getting penniless miners back home to their families, although perhaps he was one of the reasons they were without funds.

Smith ruled Denver and Creede, but it was his takeover of Skagway that made him a legend in his own time. He abhorred violence despite living in the roughest of times on a wild and lawless frontier. He feared no one and managed to hold his own no matter what. He killed no one until the fatal shootout with Frank H. Reid on the docks of Skagway.

Although not physically strong Smith made a commanding appearance. He was of medium height, dark complexion, with snapping black eyes, and in his later years sported an exceptionally dark beard. He had a pleasant baritone voice, smoked large black cigars and as early as his days on the Chisholm Trail wore a heavy gold watch and chain. In his later years he added a diamond stickpin. Described as being dapper, slender, genteel and glib, he was extremely agile and an expert horseman. He was considered by many as a good fellow, but a badcitizen, at odds with the law, which pursued him in endless fashion. Yet he was also the law's best friend.

He was an extrovert, a man of remarkable generalship anddiplomacy, at times suave and urbane with a keen sense of humor. A many sided rascal he was beyond doubt the most artful brigand of his generation, the unchallenged King of Bunco throughout the West.

According to those who knew him his various acts of kindness would do credit to any man. No one in actual need was ever turned down, no matter Soapy's finances at the time. There were legions who blessed his name for his championing the cause of the outcast.

It was often said that there was not a city in the country where one couldn't find someone who would tell of the good act that Jeff Smith had done for him.

Bobby Sheldon, who as a 14-year old newsboy witnessed the Frank ReidSoapy Smith shootout on the Skagway dock, describes the incident to Soapy's grandson, Randy Smith. This is the only known meeting, other than when Soapy's widow and their oldest son visited Skagway shortly after the shooting, that a member of the Smith family has talked with an actual witness to the affair. Young Jeff Smith, Soapy's great grandson, and Randy's wife were also present at the meeting. - H. Clifford

A great deal of Soapy's success was traceable to his sensitivity to public opinion. While everyone in Denver, Creede and Skagway knew that he was the leader of the underworld, he was also acknowledged as a guardian of the law. Thus, almost any discussion set on removing Soapy wound up with most admitting, "but you have to hand it to him, he does a lot of good, too."

He cared little for money. He simply liked to run things his own way. Yet he never missed an opportunity to separate the gullible from their ready cash as long as they were visitors and not a resident of whatever town he resided in at the time. Neither did he ever pass up an opportunity to preach and practice the gospel of kindness and compassion.

Beyond a doubt he was the greatest con man of all times. He learned the soap trick from its inventor and improved upon it. He was the master of the shell game, the standby of all buncos.

He stated "I am no ordinary gambler. Ordinary gamblers hazard their own money in an attempt to win. When I stake money it is a sure thing that I will win."

This despite his weakness for and often big loser at Faro, better known as "Bucking the Tiger." It was the one game he could not master.

This then was Jefferson Randolph Smith - better known to all as "Soapy" Smith.

CHAPTER 1
HERE COMES SOAPY.

Jefferson Randolph Smith was born in Noonan, Georgia on November 2, 1860. He died on July 8, 1898 as a result of a shootout with Frank H. Reid on the Skagway waterfront, although there is some doubt that Reid fired the fatal shots.

Jeff Smith was the son of an old and illustrious southern family, who found their way of life disrupted by the Civil War and the invasion of carpetbaggers after the conflict.

His mother, the former Emily Edmondson, was a southern beauty and a bible-toting Christian. His grandmother was known as the Belle of Virginia and the Pride of Georgia.

His father was an erudite attorney, one of the most honored in the community but addicted to drink. Two of Jeff's uncles were attorneys. There was also a doctor, a minister and a farmer.

Jeff was the oldest of five children, the others being Eva, Emma Lou and Bascom. Bascom was even more of a rascal and rogue than Jeff but not as adroit and at times caused Jeff considerable trouble.

The Smiths were a family of culture and Jeff often quoted from the classics and the bible. At one time he considered going into the ministry.

He was brought up during the time that the business motto for all, from the board rooms and banks of Wall Street to the small time operators on the frontier, was "get it while the getting is good." Jeff did his best.

At 10 years of age Jeff was doing the same work as the men on the plantation, and was delighted with the outdoor life. He was shrewd and energetic as well as a good manager and hard worker.

In the mid-1870s the family moved to Temple, Texas and later settled in Round Rock where his mother went into the hotel business, operating a two-story frame hotel in

Jeff Smith as a child in Georgia. The family moved to Texas as Jeff became a teenager and where he grew into manhood. - J.J. Smith Collection.

1

the 100 block of West Baghdad Street, as his father had become a hopeless alcoholic. It was here that Jeff garnered the traits that were to be his guidelines for the rest of his life. His job was to meet the incoming trains and steer the people who got off to his mother's hotel. Most were delighted to learn from young Jeff that the hotel in Round Rock compared to the famed Delmonicos and that they could buy goods at honest prices, especially after having been royally fleeced in other frontier towns.

If there were complaints — as generally was the case — they were not against the good-looking lad with the wavy hair and innocent gray eyes who steered them to the hotel. No one considered him a party to the deception.

Round Rock was in the midst of the great cattle country and Jeff learned to ride at an early age and soon took part in the drives, first into Missouri and later on the Chisholm Trail and on to Kansas as they veered in the direction of Dodge City, Abilene and Wichita.

Here too, is where he learned to handle a deck of cards and a gun, becoming one of the best shots and fastest draws among those he associated with. Years later it was stated that he was much faster on the draw than most professional gun slingers of the time.

Soapy lacked the killer instinct, however, and when he used a gun it was solely in the act of self defense and to maim rather than kill.

It was on the cattle drives that Jeff became acquainted with Joe Simons, who was to become his closest friend and companion.

One such drive ended in Abilene where Smith lost a month's pay in a shell game at the circus. Although he was upset at losing, it was a game that changed the entire course of his life. Jeff decided that gaming was much better than riding the trail as a cowboy and parted from Simons and used his riding skills to join the circus.

He made friends with his nemesis, one Clubfoot Hall, who took him on as a shill and taught him the fundamentals of the walnut shells and elusive pea. It wasn't long until Jeff was as skilled as his teacher. The circus reached Leadville, Colo. during the height of its glory days as a mining camp in the 1870s. Jeff left the circus and set up his keister at the corner of 3rd and Harrison Sts. In no time at all he was drawing the curious like bees to honey. His spiel was perfect and his voice was unmatched by any other bunco artist.

One day the crowds in Leadville did not come. They were across the street watching a man selling soap. Jeff was enthralled, and soon joined the throng. He watched as the man apparently wrapped large and small denomination bills in with some of the bars of soap, tossed them into a basket, offering the crowd the opportunity to purchase the soap at a $1 a bar with the possibility of winning as much as $100. The

Jeff Smith (left) and his closest boyhood friend, Joe Simons, as they appeared while riding the Chisholm Trail. Smith, even in the early days, sported a gold watch and chain. In later years he added a diamond stickpin. - Clifford Collection.

peddler was V. Bullock "Old Man" Taylor, inventor of the soap game. Jeff decided this was better than the shell game, and soon gave Taylor the grifter's signal. After disposing of his soap, with nary a customer getting more than $5, Taylor folded shop, and Smith followed him back to his hotel.

After a lengthy but convincing discussion Jeff made a deal. He would serve as a capper, receive one of the $100 packages and call attention to his luck, thus encouraging others to make a purchase. It wasn't long before Taylor was teaching Jeff how to palm the large bills, never wrapping them in the packages, and in a short while young Jeff Smith was as gifted as his mentor.

Tiring of Leadville, Taylor moved on to Minneapolis, and after a short stay, Smith also packed up and moved to Denver where he set up at 17th and Market - which later was to become his favorite place to hang out.

Jeff fared poorly in Denver until another con man mentioned that he looked too young to be taken seriously and suggested that he grow a beard. That was the making of Jeff Smith.

Being a master of slight of hand, Smith became am expert in deception and would attracted large crowds. So deft was Jeff in removing the bills while wrapping the soap that none other than his cappers garnered the large notes. On occasion others received $5 or $10, mainly as a come-on.

Smith reportedly got the name "Soapy" in Denver when he was arrested for selling soap without a license. Upon being booked, the police officer making the report and who knew Jeff well, had forgotten his first name. Too embarrassed to ask, he booked him as "Soapy" Smith. The name stuck. Although none of his close friend addressed him by other than "Jeff." The prefix of "Soapy" was used in the sense that President Roosevelt was called "Teddy."

Jeff became so successful, not only with the soap game, but also at the shell game, cards, dice and other slight of hand tricks, that it wasn't long before other con men came around and introduced themselves to Soapy. One was Lemuel Baggs, better known as Doc Baggs, the premier con-man of the era and famous for his selling of "gold bricks." He later became Soapy's top capper. Another was Canada Bill (William Jones), who according to Pinkerton detectives, was the outstanding swindler of the time. The two took a liking to young Smith and took him under their wing. Needless to say, Jeff Smith was a quick learner.

4

CHAPTER 2
WEDDING BELLS

Some time after arriving in Denver, Jeff married Anna Nielson on Feb. 1, 1886. She was a singer and actress known as "Allie" at the Palace Theater in Denver, a notorious place resembling the cabarets in New York. It was operated by William Barkley "Bat" Masterson also known as Bartholomew Masterson. Jeff and Bat became close friends.

The Palace was where the "big names" in the entertainment world appeared when they visited Denver. Its reputation, however, untouched Anna. A Rocky Mountain News reporter, W.F. Hayes stated, "even the most depraved would not dare to offend her. She received the homage of chivalry from men who had forgotten that it ever existed."

Soapy's and Anna's romance started as a result of an attempt by a Palace patron, in his cups, who sought to be familiar with Anna against her protest as she was leaving the stage one evening. Jeff, who was in the balcony at the time, saw her struggling and lost no time in reaching her.

Two weeks later the doctor told her assailant that he could return to work although he still had marks from the melee.

After their marriage, Soapy set Anna up in a elegant cottage on Capitol Hill's Pearl Street, far from the hustle and bustle of downtown Denver. He kept her away from his business operations at all times.

Good or bad, Soapy did not mind what the press had to say about him personally, but was very protective of his wife. Some time after their marriage, an article, which he felt was derogatory to Anna, appeared in the Rocky Mountain News, resulting in Jeff sending her back to her family home in St. Louis. After seeing her off on the train, Smith headed for the News Building, accompanied by Banjo Parker, who weighed a mere 250 pounds.

As Col. John Arkins, president and publisher of the News, left the building Soapy called and started towards him. As the Colonel turned Smith threw up his left hand to shove him back and then hit him over the head two or three times with his cane. Col. Arkins fell and Soapy hit him a couple more blows with his fist and then kicked him as he lay in the gutter. Parker stood by and watched in amazement, but made no attempt to join in the fracas. His size discouraged any bystanders from trying to assist.

Soapy turned and walked away. Col. Arkins suffered a fractured skull and was treated by a nearby physician before being taken to the hospital.

Smith was arrested a short time later, quietly walking to jail with the officer, posted bond and was on his way. The News in a story the

**Wedding photo of Jefferson Randolph Smith and his bride
Anna Nielson. They were married in early February 1886 and
made their first home in Denver. As Jeff prospered and moved
from city to city, Anna returned to her family home in St.
Louis. - J.J. Smith Collection.**

next day called him an "assassin" and stated that Soapy and "his mob"
had attacked the Colonel.

At a preliminary court hearing six days later, Smith was charged
with assault to do bodily harm. He took time to make it clear to the
court the reason for the attack. The case never came to trial.

Jeff's and Anna's three children, Jefferson R. Jr., James and Eva
were born in St. Louis. He invested much of his winnings in diamonds
which he sent her and which remained in her possession. On his frequent visits to St. Louis he had the habit of tossing his "cash roll"
behind a painting which hung from a plate rail on the wall of the family
home at 917 Locust St. Despite the many visits, he never retrieved any
of the money and Anna saved most of the funds for the future.

To the end of his days no matter his current financial condition,
Jeff regularly sent money to his mother and his wife, and closed his
letters devotedly. This was their only income as Soapy's father, although
still alive at age 87 when Jeff died, was a chronic alcoholic.

Years after Jeff's death, Anna married a St. Louis policeman. It
is believed that they moved to Milwaukee and that she died and was
buried there.

Sixteen Smith family members as well as Reid relatives were on hand in Skagway on July 8, 1998 to mark the 100th Anniversary of the Reid/Smith shootout. They, along with Smith followers, authors and others from throughout the country took part in the program. It including a symposium on "who killed Soapy", which came to the conclusion that it was not Frank Reid. There was also a reenactment of the shooting on the waterfront as well as dedication of a plaque at the site.

CHAPTER 3
SOAPY TO THE RESCUE

One of Soapy's most daring swindles was that of prize fighter Bob Fitzsimmons, world middleweight boxing champion, who later won the heavyweight crown from Gentleman Jim Corbett in a fight in Carson City, Nev. in 1898.

"Ruby Bob" as he was known, and his wife who acted as his manager, arrived in Denver well healed with cash after a successful defense of his middleweight title against Tommy Ryan in California. They put up in the Windsor Hotel and soon met up with Reverend John Bowers, Soapy's capable aide. He introduced himself as Collis P. Huntington of San Francisco, president of the Southern Pacific Railroad.

It wasn't long before Fitzsimmons was escorted to the luxurious "stock exchange" offices of Jefferson Randolph Smith. He was greatly impressed and in a short time the group adjourned to Smith's private office with its massive mahogany sideboard stocked with fine liquors, and incidentally an innocent looking card table was nearby.

They soon engaged in a friendly card game, in which one of the greatest prize fighters of all time won initially, but soon lost all his cash along with his diamond studded championship belt. He was flat broke.

Huntington (Bowers) also "lost" and explained that he would gladly make good on Fitz's losses including funds to reclaim the belt since he was responsible for getting Fitzsimmons in the game.

"Meet me at my private car at the depot this evening and I will give you $5,000 and the pick of diamonds twice the value of your losses for your wife," he added.

Fitzsimmons arrived at the depot at the appointed hour and asked directions to Mr. Huntington's private car. He was informed that there was no such car at the depot. Ruby Bob was furious, but there was little he could do. He returned to the Windsor, vowing vengeance on Smith in the morning.

Upon arriving at Soapy's "office," which had gone through one of Smith's renown "quick changes" he was greeted by an elderly Chinese who opened the door of a bedroom filled with definitely feminine furnishing. He exclaimed "Missy no home, missy go work." He shut the door gently in the face of a furious Fitzsimmons.

The championship belt was never found, and it is almost certain that Smith had the diamonds removed to add to his wife's collection and most likely the gold buckle was melted down.

Few things really bothered Smith, but one that did was the nickel-in-the-slot music boxes, forerunner of modern day juke boxes. During his travels Soapy learned that by hammering a nickel a bit, making it just a shade wider than normal it would jam up the works and play the same number indefinitely. Generally just as he left a place where the music box had played too loud and too long for Soapy's liking, he would insert one of his "enlarged" nickels that he always carried. One time at the Denver Union Station he jammed the music box so that it played "Maggie Murphy" for six solid hours before mechanics could removed the jammed coin.

An occasion in which Soapy could have killed a rival should such be his mien occurred in Pocatello, Idaho. When he and his followers hit the road during one of Denver's "reform" periods, they visited Salt Lake City and Ogden only to be as unwelcome in each city as he was in Denver.

The next stop was Pocatello which at the time was a wide open railroad town with a tough area on the east side of the tracks. Here gambling was rampant and the red-light district boasted of more than 100 women. It looked like easy picking for one such as Soapy.

Word of Smith's plan to move on from Odgen to Pocatello proceeded him and he debarked from the train to a surprise greeting from an old acquaintance, not a friendly one, however.

Back in early 1890s when Smith was just coming into power in Denver, a brash, pugnacious young shell-game artist named Kelly and known as the "Rincon Kid" breezed into town. At first Soapy paid little attention to the newcomer perfectly willing to let him operate as long as Kelly stayed within bounds.

The newcomer, however, gaining confidence, made one mistake. He dared to move onto Seventeenth Street, which Soapy considered his own exclusive territory. The matter was settled without violence, but with a stern warning from Soapy, along with an assist from a "friendly" police department. The "Rincon Kid" and his gang moved on, threatening to get even.

Soapy paid little attention as to Kelly's destination, and was greatly surprised when he disembarked from the train at Pocatello and was greeted by the "Rincon Kid" and his gang with weapons drawn and the warning to Soapy to keep moving.

Smith refused to budge, and despite Kelly's gang having their weapons in hand, he was able to draw his own pistol, fire with accuracy and hit Sam Beecher, Kelly's aide, in the leg.

All dove for cover, and continued firing at each other for quite a period without further damage. There was much relief on both sides when the local police arrived, ordered them to give up their weapons and put them all under arrest.

After a lengthy discussion, only Soapy was jailed. He received a speedy trial and was found not guilty on the basis that he fired in self defense. The "Rincon Kid" and his gang were put on the first southbound train, and Soapy and his followers on the northbound to Spokane. There was no doubt that Smith was quick and accurate enough with firearms to have hit and killed Kelly or any of his gang with that first shot had he so desired. Likewise, all were better gunmen than they showed in the "friendly" shootout.

Smith and his followers spent considerable time in the Northwest without stirring up too much trouble, and finally as things cooled down, returned to Denver.

Soapy was back in power in Denver. There soon was a major decrease in violent crimes as the police counted on him to keep things "civilized." Smith also made generous contributions to churches and the poor which gave him a Robin Hood image. His various cons continued to working well.

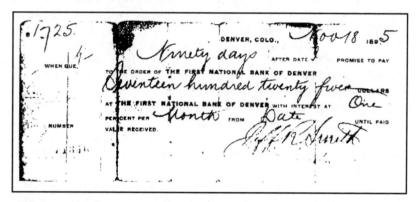

Jeff Smith knew how to ingratiate himself in the right circles in Denver. Discovered among his papers discovered after his death was this promissory note which, having been accepted without endorsement, proved that his credit was good among business leaders. - Clifford Collection.

Smith's pet anathema was meanness and viciousness in any form and of these he was wholly intolerant and did not hesitate to help the police in wiping them out if he could

His most conspicuous act in this field was the single handed raid on the Gleason Detective Agency in Denver and which brought him the unique reputation of being a public benefactor.

Soapy preyed only on those out-of-towners who had the cash to lose. Not so with the Gleason Agency, which according to the police themselves, was a shady operation specializing in blackmail. Gleason detectives spent their time prying into the personal affairs and stirring up scandals among some of Denver's most prominent citizens. Police had been unsuccessful in their investigations.

The Gleason Agency made one mistake. They started tailing Smith and interfering in Soapy's business. Soapy did nothing, biding his time which came in a most unusual manner.

The Denver newspapers carried a story that the Gleason Agency had used drugs and liquor trying to force a false confession from a pretty young servant girl to the effect that she was plotting to rob a wealthy Denver matron of her jewels.

Soapy read the article and felt that this was the time to strike. Single handed he took off with the announcement to his followers that the "Gleason Detective Agency is going out of business today."

Smith stormed in the Gleason office, gun in hand, before Gleason and his staff could make a move. Soapy literally destroyed the interior, firing shots at random but being careful not to hit anyone. One detective took a swing at Smith, giving him a beautiful shiner, but that was all.

With the entire staff fully cowed, Soapy ransacked files, gathered up all the papers in sight including secret records. He added insult to injury by taking the detective badges, even those worn by the staff.

Wearing a black eye and broad grin, his arms full of papers and books, Jeff left the offices and sauntered down the street.

A few yards away he encountered Police Captain Thomas Russell, called by citizens who heard the ruckus. Smith related what had happened and stated that he intended to burn all of the papers. Capt. Russell, who had been on the Gleason trail, offered no opposition and cheerfully commended Smith.

Returning to his headquarters, Soapy passed out the Gleason badges as souvenirs and burned all the papers. He also found himself the recipient of plaudits from both police and grateful citizens. As the story spread, he became a popular hero and a citizen entitled to respect to the extent that he was asked to assist in the next election. He was accepted into business groups that had fought or ignored him in the past. Even some of the upper crust ladies clubs that had ignored his wife looked favorably towards him.

11

CHAPTER 4
CREEDE

Jeff was doing well in Denver when Nicholas C. Creede made one of the West's greatest silver finds in the Colorado mountains. Word of the discovery spread like wildfire. It was too good for Soapy to pass up as by 1892 the town named after Creede had become the richest and wildest of Colorado's mining towns.

Creede had become so wild that Cy Warman, editor of the Creede Candle, described the community as follows:

"It's day all day in the daytime.
And there is no night in Creede."

Booming Creede was too new and raw to have much of a civic organization and at the time of Soapy's arrival had two bosses, Bob Ford in his Exchange Saloon and Bat Masterson in the Watrous Saloon. Bat and Soapy were friends of long standing, but neither got along with Ford.

Smith started his Creede career at a slow pace with the shell

William Barclay "Bat" Masterson, was a close friend of Soapy's in both Denver and Creede. They kept in close contact during their travels. Public Library, Western History Dept.

game and his favorite soap gimmick. Soon the so-called King of the Thimble-ringers was on his way to taking over. At the time more than half of the population in Creede was made up of bunco artists, mining sharks, saloon keepers, pick-pockets, dance hall girls, professional gamblers and assorted riffraff. More colorful characters included Whiskey Johnny who packed kegs of cheap watered down booze to the high remote mines on burros and sold it at scandalous prices. Lady gamblers included Poker Alice Tubbs, Creede Lilly and Kilarney Kate.

One of Soapy's first steps was establishment of some sort of government. He called together a group of citizens and businessmen and stated that if they would set up a government he would maintain law and order by controlling the rough element.

Other than for Soapy, there was no law in Creede. One of his first steps was to send for his brother-in-law, John Light, a former Texas Ranger and well respected town marshal. With Light came Smith's boyhood chum, Joe Simons, who once again became his partner and closest companion.

When friends from Denver dropped in, Soapy entertained them royally and had the habit of walking them through town, pointing out its highlights but also showing them to the rougher element so that they were recognized as friends of Soapy's and were to be left alone as far as the rough stuff was concerned.

Although Smith took Robert N. (Bob) Ford in as a partner in the Petrified Man display in Creede the two did not get along. - Clifford Collection.

It wasn't long before Bob Ford, who felt he bossed the town, uttered an ultimatum to Smith giving him the choice of getting out of town on his own or in a pine box. This is what Jeff had been waiting for. He visited Ford in the latter's private office and convinced Jesse James' killer that there was enough in Creede for both and that Ford would not regret joining forces with him. Smith soon cut Ford in on what was to be the bunco artist's most audacious scheme.

A short time earlier, a local gambler Bob Fitzsimmons (no relation to the boxer), had discovered a full size figure of a man molded out of cement and plaster in a Denver junkyard. He mentioned the fact to Smith and Soapy jumped at the opportunity. He had the figure packed and shipped as machinery to a mining claim in Creede. The figure was partially buried in a gulch forking Willow Creek and Soapy sat back and waited.

Within a few days another prospector, J.J. Dore, stumbled on to the figure and rushed to town with the news. It wasn't long before the discovery. initially known as "McGinty" but soon dubbed "Colonel Stone" became big news throughout the area. The Denver Rocky Mountain News headlined the discovery in the April ll, 1892 issue, "J.J. Dore Finds the Body of Petrified Man Near Creede." Smith "purchased" the stone figure from Dore and Fitzsimmons, as noted in the Creede Candle.

A WONDER

THE

PETRIFIED MAN

Discovered near Creede, Colo., April 9, 1892

A petrifaction as natural as life, showing a fine specimen of manhood; every muscle, and even the pores of the skin are plainly seen by the naked eye. Parts of the petrifaction have been analyzed by the most skeptical, and it has been pronounced genuine by all. $1,000 to any one proving to the contrary. Skeptics, Doctors and all Scientific men are especially invited.

ON EXHIBITION AT

914 SEVENTEENTH ST.

Admission, 10 Cents.

Advertisement which appeared in several Creede publications for Soapy's Petrified Man display Clifford Collectio

"Jeff Smith has purchased the petrified man, and will travel with him. The price was $3,000. Jeff paid the money this morning and went down to get possession. Four others claimed ownership, and it required some lively discussion with fists and guns to get away with it."

Col. Stone was moved to Soapy's temporary headquarters in the Vaughn Hotel barroom. Well aware of the attention received, Smith soon quashed the belief that it was the body of one of General Fremont's men who passed through the valley in 1842. Instead, after "much scientific research," he came up with the theory that it was possibly a "Prehistoric Man - The Missing Link" and had it put on display under eerie flickering kerosene lighting in Bob Ford's saloon. Soapy's spiel was even more spellbinding that any of his soap pitches. Hundreds came, and Soapy earned thousands of dollars. It also put Ford under Smith's control. It wasn't much later that Smith and his partner, Joe Simons opened the elegant Orleans Club down the street from Ford's place. At the same time Smith let it be known that he was the boss of Creede.

Later Col. Stone was leased out to P.T. Barnum for a nationwide tour. As it began to disintegrate from hard usage Smith sold it to R.V. Ellison of Hilliard, Wash. It was last seen years ago unclaimed and flaking away in the Hilliard freight shed.

This certainly was Smith's most profitable hoax of all time so much so that in November of the same year a similar "discovery" was made by others in a cave in New Mexico. The finders were not as financially successful as Smith, but the cave of the New Mexico find came to be known as the Carlsbad Caverns.

By April 1892, after Smith had taken over control of Creede, Parson Tom Uzzell, known as "Parson Tom" and who Jeff had known in Leadville and later in Denver, came to town. For lack of a better place to deliver his sermons, he setup on a pool table in Bat Masterson's saloon. Following the sermon, Masterson suggested that a collection

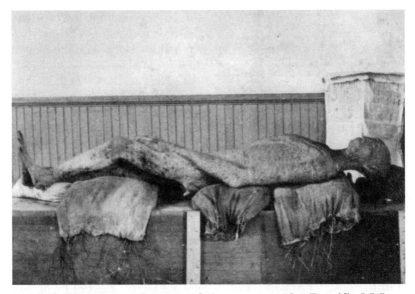

One of the greatest hoaxes of the era was the Petrified Man, which drew thousands of spectators and enriched the cofers of Soapy Smith. P.T. Barnum later leased it from Soapy. Later it was stored in a railroad depot in Washington State. - Clifford Collection.

be taken and turned over to Parson Tom. When Smith learned of this visit by Rev. Uzzell, he asked why he chose a saloon for his sermon. Rev. Uzzell explained that there was no church or suitable hall for such in Creede.

Smith assured him that such would be corrected and swung into action. First he contacted Masterson and inquired as to the amount of the collection. Bat stated that he had no idea but was certain that it was not enough to build a church. They went into action.

Early the next morning the parson, sans pants, was banging on Soapy's door. Someone had broken into his room and stolen his trousers and money during the night.

Soapy appeared enraged, but told the preacher not to worry that he would take care of things. Unknown to Rev. Uzzell, Smith and Masterson had plotted against Preacher Tom. They had Joe Palmer, one of Soapy's henchmen, break into the parson's hotel room and steal his pants and money. At Soapy's suggestion they agreed to matched the collection amount.

The next morning Rev. Uzzell was once again knocked at Soapy's door. Not only had the pants and money been returned but the funds had grown to $700.

Thomas A. "Parson Tom" Uzzell crossed paths with Jeff Smith on many occasions starting in Leadville and continuing until Smith headed north to Alaska. Soapy helped Rev. Uzzell raise funds for many of his churches and preached a sermon in the People's Tabernacle in Denver. - Clifford Collection.

By evening the townspeople of Creede had heard of Soapy's action and his stock with the church groups soared.

The church was built and the next Sunday Smith and his followers attended the first service and were most generous with their contributions to the collection plate.

The business community of Creede tolerated Smith, and in some cases applauded him because he seemed to bring order out of chaos as was often the case when men preferred order to liberty, which was confused with anarchy.

All of Smith's men respected him and he was fond of them. But Simons was the closest. The two had punched cattle together in Texas, had "skinned" many a sucker over the years and now were partners in the plush Orleans Club in Creede.

When Jeff learned that his closest friend, had pneumonia the scourge of the mining camps and fatal in high altitudes, he did everything that he could to save Joe's life. As Simons lay dying he told Soapy he didn't want any preachin' as his sendoff. "Just lay me out and wish me good health on the other side of the range, if there is any other side." His death left Soapy disconsolate. Many say he was never the same.

The Creede Candle stated that when the casket was lowered into the grave Smith addressed the mourners. "The man whom we have just laid to rest was the best friend I ever had. You all knew him. Did any of you ever know him to do a thing that wasn't square with his friends? No. I thought not. Neither did I. The best we can do now is to wish him the best there is in the land beyond the range, or if there is any hereafter. Joe didn't think there was and I don't know anything about it. Friends, I ain't much of a speaker, but Joe was my friend and all he wanted was for us to gather at his grave and drink to his health when he was gone. Let us do it."

An angry mob gathered in front of Bob Ford's Exchange Club in Creede following Ford's death. Smith restored order, preventing a riot. Ford's original saloon had been replaced by a tent following the first of several fires that destroyed most of downtown Creede. Smith's Orleans Club was nearby, but

Following Simon's death and burial Soapy displayed his emotions, taking the death of Simons very hard and appeared moody and lonely after the loss.

Billy DeVere, "The Tramp Poet of the Rockies," immortalized the event with a long, touching sentimental poem entitled,"Jeff and Joe."

On June 7, 1892 Smith found himself in a position to show his authority and law abiding leadership when Edward Capehart (Ed) O'Kelley shot Robert N. (Bob) Ford,Jesse James' killer, in Ford's Exchange Club. At the time, the Exchange was housed in a tent as the original Club had burned in Creede's first major fire. Soapy's Orleans Club nearby escaped the blaze.

Following the shooting, O'Kelley, much to his surprise, did not find himself a hero for killing Ford which he imagined would be the case. Earlier the Vigilantes had ousted Ford from Creede over the objections of many and he had talked his way back into town.

Instead, an angry mob of citizens gathered and O'Kelley would have found himself dangling from the end of a rope had not an orator with the ability to sway even an angry mob, stepped forward and demanded that the law be allowed to take its course.

That orator was Jefferson Randolph Smith. If his object was to prevent a lynching, he was successful. If it was to prove that Jeff Smith was on the side of law and order, in that too, he was successful. O'Kelley did not hang. He was tried and given a life sentence. After spending 10 years behind bars O'Kelley, who had also murdered another man in Pueblo in 1891, a year before he shot Ford, was given a full pardon. He was killed in a gun fight with a police officer in Oklahoma City in June, 1904.

Never one to bet on a dead horse, Smith saw that with the upcoming "death of silver" and having seen his closest friend, Joe Simons, pass away he decided to move on. Creede, which in 1892 suffered the first of several disastrous fires, never regained its former glory.

As Smith sold the Orleans Club and headed back to Denver, one of the Creede's leaders remarked, "Soapy, we are going to miss you like a steam calliope at a circus, but things are settling down now and we are going to run the town along new lines."

Denver, once again was wide open and Jeff was back in the saddle again with his fabulous Tivoli at 17th and Market Sts.

CHAPTER 5

BATTLE OF DENVER.

During his days in Denver Soapy was often called upon by Officer Sullivan, the depot police patrolman, to "lend a hand." This especially when young mothers, with two or three youngsters in tow, arrived in the "big city" without funds or return tickets, seeking their husbands who were mining in Aspen, Leadville, or was it Central City? They weren't quite sure, in as much as he had moved around so much seeking the elusive precious metals.

Officer Sullivan, always on hand during such emergencies, knew just what to do. Soapy was called upon for assistance, and he always came through. Sullivan would get word to Smith with the same confidence of a favorable response as he could expect when he pulled his signal for the patrol wagon.

On one such call, Soapy arrived as expected, but without as much as a nickel to his name. He was stone broke.

Just then one of the two youngsters that the young wife had in tow, with tears in his eyes, asked Soapy, "Do you know my daddy, mister?"

This hit Smith like a rock. With a voice choking and doubtful, he replied, "Yes, he sent me some money for you but I forgot it. You sit here with your mother and I will get it for you."

As he strode back up 17th Street Soapy was in one of his most dangerous moods. He picked up a .45 to go with his white handled derringer which he always carried. He was mumbling, "Of all the times, not a dollar, not a damn dollar. Oh hell." Soapy headed for the Arcade, one of the larger gambling clubs in Denver, one in which he was very well known.

As he entered he slammed the door behind him with a bang, drawing everyone's attention. He had drawn both pistols.

"Line up — and hands up," he hissed. He then order several of the employees he knew by name to grab their handkerchiefs and fill them with all the paper money they could grab from the tables. He gave them five seconds to complete the job, or he would start shooting.

Others joined in to help. They all knew he meant business and although many were armed, none made a move for their weapons. Smith ordered them to stuff the bills in his coat pockets. Soapy ducked out the door, the doorman having conveniently disappeared, slamming it once again and headed back to the depot. No one attempted to follow.

Fifteen minutes later, Soapy was back at the depot, and with a knowing Officer Sullivan at his side handed the mother and her youngsters the handfuls of bills from his pockets.

"I'm sorry ma'am," he apologized, "for keeping you here so long. I knew where the money was, but I had quite a little distance to go and return, and then some friends kept on talking. No, ma'am. I didn't stop to count it. It just as I received it."

Officer Sullivan chuckled as he thanked Soapy, but the big chuckle came the next day, and all Denver laughed with him. A local wag, full of lilting tunes and humor, paraphrased an old song on Soapy's exploit.

> "The tables cashed, the players ceased their play.
> Their pile was gone — no longer need to stay.
> Tho the lights were bright, the hall was dreary.
> The music dead, the dancers weary.
> After Soapy went away."

Another Denver confrontation came following the election as governor of Colorado Populist David H. Waite, former Aspen newspaper publisher and Justice of The Peace.

Waite hated lawlessness and vice. He was quick on the trigger following his election when he called out the militia and vowed to break a miner's strike, even if he had to ride through blood up to his bridle - earning the nickname of "Blood Up To The Bridle" or "Bloody Bridles" Waite.

Gov. Waite next took on the corruption of Denver city officials and threatened to remove them if they did not clean up their act. He named a new police and fire commissioner and other appointees and threatened to use force to remove the incumbents who refused to budge. Gov. Waite once again called out the militia ordering them to take over City Hall.

The City Commissioners were much concerned and as was their policy when trouble arose, they called upon Jeff for help. Overnight he raised an army of some 400 men from the sporting fraternity, "borrowed" all the firearms in hardware stores and pawn shops, secured 500 pounds of dynamite and became "Colonel" Smith, directing the operation himself.

Under Smith's leadership the entire police force, along with a contingent from the fire department took over the ground floor of City Hall. Soapy and his men manned the tower and upper story windows with former miners becoming powdermen with dynamite bombs.

In the early dawn of March 15, 1894 the tramp of martial feet resounded through the downtown streets of Denver as three companies of the state national guard and a light artillery battery with cannons moved into position.

Keeping in touch with the troops from his well guarded home, Gov. Waite ordered the militia to "Take City Hall." After surveying the situation a surprised, General Brooks sent an urgent message back to

Dubbed the Battle of Denver, Jefferson Randolph Smith and his followers, including the police department and most of the city's firefighters, outwitted the Governor and Colorado National Guard in a struggle for possession of Denver City Hall. Not a shot was fired and no one was injured. Crowds gathered to cheer "Colonel" Smith as he left the building. - Denver Public Library, Western History Dept.

the Governor, "If a single shot is fired," he stated, "they will kill me instantly and they will kill you within 15 minutes. But if you say fire, we'll fire."

Action was delayed and after a lengthy conference the Governor was convinced it was best to let the courts decide the issue and some hours later the militia withdrew.

"Colonel" Jeff Smith, with rifle in his hands, made his way down the steps of City Hall to the cheers of the Denver townspeople. The bloodless war was over and Soapy was still the boss of Denver. He soon moved on however, as the courts brought about changes in the city government.

Colonel Smith's title, which he bestowed upon himself, accounted for his next venture into the military. He contacted His Excellency Don Jose de la Cruz Porfirio, President of the Republic of Mexico, who despite being a popular hero when taking office had by 1895

Soapy's acceptance by the Denver business community is noted by the Rocky Mountain News on Oct. 16 1882 at a meeting of Arapahoe County politicians in executive session. Soapy Smith is third from the left. - Clifford Collection.

become a tyrant and oppressor and was in constant trouble with unorganized guerrillas.

Posing as a distinguished American Army officer Colonel Smith wrote to Diaz, volunteering to come to Mexico with an army of 500 hardened frontier fighters to put down rebellions and lawlessness.

The letter interested the President and he invited Col. Smith to Mexico City. Accompanied by the Reverend John Bowers, his "chief diplomatic aide and advisor", they received a royal welcome.

After several days of entertainment and diplomatic dinners, Smith and His Excellency came to an agreement that Col. Smith would supply an army of 500 good fighting men. When Soapy requested $80,000 to cover training expenses, the President explained that Mexico was the land of "manana" and that the funds would be forthcoming shortly.

Try as he did, Soapy was unable to change His Excellency's mind, but did come up with $2,000 to cover "out of pocket expenses." Soapy returned to Denver, explaining to his cohorts the program was in the bag.

Unknown to Soapy, however, he had been followed by Mexican agents who investigated the colonel's career and credentials. Shortly thereafter President Diaz informed Col. Smith the deal was off.

CHAPTER 6
GOLDEN RUMORS

During the period from early 1881 to 1889, while Smith was in Colorado, repeated reports of gold strikes on the upper Yukon River kept making the rounds in Canada and the United States. Although little or practically no attention was paid to them at the time there were more than 50 prospectors from the world over in the area. Smith kept such information in the back of his mind.

Early in 1887 Captain William "Billy" Moore, who had made and lost several fortunes as a river boat captain, prospector, packer and trader, contracted to go into the Yukon Territory with a Canadian government survey party headed by William Ogilvie. Capt. Moore was to provide the know-how of packing over wilderness trails and build and navigate a barge down the Yukon River with supplies.

At the time, the favored entry into the Yukon was by the tortuous Chilkoot Trail, controlled by the Chilkoot Indians. Earlier Moore had heard of another route from the head of Skagway Bay, some 600 feet lower in elevation. He was determined to find the route. Accompanied by a native guide Skookum Jim, Capt. Moore sought the new route while Ogilvie and the main party traveled via Chilkoot Pass to Lake Bennett, headwaters of the Yukon River.

It took Moore many days longer than the others to reach Bennett over the uncharted, perilous switchbacks and precipitous hillsides and canyons. Despite the hardships, Captain Billy was most enthusiastic about the new route. It was named White Pass after Thomas White, Canadian Minister of the Interior.

Concluding his explorations with Ogilivy, Capt. Moore, recalled

Skookum Jim was a key figure in the Klondike gold rush. He accompanied Capt. Billy Moore when Moore discovered the White Pass route over the mountains. Later he was one of three prospectors who discovered gold in Bonanza Creek starting the Klondike stampede. - Clifford Collection.

23

that on many occasions he had seen Indians coming out from the Yukon with large quantities of gold. He was convinced that eventually there would be a discovery and following gold rush. With this in mind he came to the conclusion that White Pass would be the route to the gold fields and that Skagway Bay would be the ideal entry port.

As Ogilvie recalled later, the old man's imagination was most inspired. "Every night during the two months he remained with us, he would picture the tons of yellow dust yet to be found in the Yukon Valley. He felt Skagway Bay would be the entry point and White Pass would reverberate with the rumble of railway trains carrying supplies."

Captain Moore returned to what is now Skagway, and on October 20, 1884, staked out and recorded a claim of 160 acres. He pitched a tent on a small knoll along side a creek to become the first white settler although in the past Indians had visited the area to hunt and fish. He replaced the tent with a log cabin for his family prior to the first winter. With his son Ben,

Captain William "Billy" Moore made and lost several fortunes. He faced another when the first Klondike stampeders hijacked his claim which became the town of Skagway. Later he was reimbursed by the courts for 25 percent of the assessed value of the improved property. - Clifford Collection.

he started construction of a sawmill and a pier on the shallow tide flats. This not only to enable him to land equipment and supplies, but also because this location would be the most logical for a town to serve the route to the Yukon. His townsite" was known as Skagus, Mooreville, Skaguay and finally Skagway.

His nearest neighbors were Indians at Smuggler's Cove, and Sam Heron who ran the Healy and Wilson Trading Post at Dyea, about six miles away. Haines Mission, 16 miles distant, was the only other settlement in the area.

Over the ensuing years individual prospectors and others made use of Moore's primitive facilities as they headed for the Yukon. He made several unsuccessful attempts to borrow money to develop his

Skagway venture, but with his poor financial background he was unsuccessful. In later years he was able to obtain limited funds and used them to improve the trail and wharf.

On May 20, 1894, more than two years prior to the major discovery of gold in the Thron Duick, which became Clondyke and eventually Klondike, Inspector Charles Constantine of the North West Mounted Police was sent into the Yukon to determine what would be required to reinforce the Government's authority on this northern frontier. On his return to Ottawa Constantine recommended an allotment of 50 men. Despite his report he was sent back to the Yukon in July 1895 with a contingent of only 19 men. He immediately started work on a fort for the first Mounted Police post in the Yukon. Thus the Canadians were well prepared when the cry of "Gold" was heard in August 1896. By 1898 the initial unit had swelled to 285 men.

In 1895 some promising gold discoveries were made in the Forty Mile Creek area, resulting in an increase in interest in the northland. In February 1895 the first group of prospectors, seven Californians with some five tons of equipment, arrived in the Skagway area aboard the Rustler and were directed by Capt. Moore to the trail over the White Pass. They were the first of thousands to follow.

CHAPTER 7

WASHINGTON D.C.

Remembering the rumors from the Yukon, Smith in 1895 went to Washington D.C to visit his cousin, Edwin "Bobo" Smith, an editor and influential newspaper man on the staff of the Washington Post. Although the Klondike strike had not taken place it had become fairly well known that there was gold to be found in Alaska and the Yukon and Soapy wanted to be in on the ground floor.

Inside Jeff felt that perhaps there was a life for him in legitimate business. He revealed that the purpose of his visit to Washington was to obtain a government concession for property on which to build a legitimate hotel in the far north at St. Michael near the mouth of the Yukon. Perhaps this would be the opportunity to make a strike that would provide for him and his family for the rest of his life.

In Washington he hobnobbed with statesmen and government officials and was accepted into the social circles of the national capitol. Here he met W.F. Hayes, a well-known New York writer, who did a lengthy interview with Smith for the New York World. Richard Harding Davis, noted foreign correspondent, was another who wrote about Soapy during his Washington stay.

Davis was a great lover of humanity, its faults as well as its follies, and he was delightfully entertained by Smith, who was full of interest, humor and anecdotes. Jeff was outspoken and unaffected but refused to comment on anything that put him in a favorable light. Although he seemed to be frank and spoke his mind without fear of suspicion. He was relaxed and at ease and Davis, according to Hayes, by shrewd, discreet questions was able to bring out many facts of his character which possibly not even Soapy was aware of.

Hawes later reported that the one great quality which he unwittingly discovered and which doubtless proved Smith's great ally in every game, was his profound knowledge of human nature, which greatly impressed Davis. It showed that Jeff was a man, and that he had the qualities that made for great executive ability, backed by more than ordinary education, although he was largely self-taught. Another light in his character that Davis brought out was his deep and tender affection for his wife and children.

Smith defended his profession as a gambler, which in that era was a well respected occupation.

Davis during the interview culled out some of Smith's quaint philosophies and later put them down in articles he wrote, such as:

"A gambler is one who teaches and illustrates the folly of avarice. He is a non-ordained preacher on the vagaries of fortune and

26

45825 A.G.O.

War Department,

ADJUTANT GENERAL'S OFFICE,

Washington,   January 26, 1898.

J. R. Smith Esq.,

Care E. B. Smith, Washington Post,

Washington, D. C.

Sir:-

I have the honor to inform you that a suitable location for
the business purposes of your company, as far as grounds, etc.,
available permit, on the military reservation of Fort St. Michael,
Alaska, has been approved by the Secretary of War, and the papers
forwarded to the Commanding.Officer at that point, with instructions that, upon presentation of this letter, he shall without
delay proceed to stake out the grounds, etc., necessary for your
business, under the enclosed regulations, and permit you to enter
upon and use them, pending the completion of the formal permit by
the signature of the Secretary of War and seal of the Department.

Very respectfully,

[signature]

Adjutant General.

During his stay in Washington D.C., Jeff "Soapy" Smith with
an assist by his cousin E.R. "Bobo" Smith, was sucessful in
gaining War Department approval to take over operations in
St. Michael. After further investigations, Smith decided he
could do better elsewhere and settle in Southeast Alaska.
- Clifford Collection.

how to make doubt a certainty.

"He is one who, in his amusements, eliminates the element of chance. Chance is merely the minister in his work-shop of luck. Money has no value except to back a good hand.

"A gambler is the only person who in the exercise of his profession learns how to smile in defeat, and is fearful to exult in success. The first leads to poverty, the other to jail.

"If he loses he is a pauper. If he wins he is a robber.

"He meets more men and women of morals — to hear them tell it -than are met in any other walk of life, including churches; though he listened to a few hyprocrits in his time — an unbearing penance.

"To play his game and lose is to hear the wail of the innocent." Following their meeting, Davis, one of the most astute men of the time, remarked, in referring to Jeff, "There is something good in the worst of us, and perhaps something bad in the best of us." to which he added — "and only god knows what's in the rest of us."

Smith's contacts, winning ways and influence on Washington was to be of benefit later when he went to Skagway. After a month in the East he departed from the capital requesting without success that Bobo accompany him to the far north. Such had also been the case early in his career when he was in Leadville. Jeff stated that he was going to build a hotel and run it straight, then return to Washington and establish himself as a reputable hotel owner. He invited Bobo to come up to St. Michael the next summer to join him and his family, which he said would be there.

It was Edwin "Bobo" Smith who made virtually the only comment the family recorded on the boy who became known as Soapy. In an interview published in 1920 he said:

"Jeff had a brilliant mind and could have achieved being President of the United States, even . . . with his faults.

CHAPTER 8

A COUPLE OF OLD SEA CAPTAINS.

Jeff stopped over in St.Louis to visit with his family before heading West. He visited Denver and then went on to Alaska.

He sailed for St. Michael on the Lakme but was not pleased with the bleak Yukon River delta town, in that most of the traffic up the Yukon was freight rather than passengers or prospectors.

Never one to pass up an opportunity, however, Jeff Smith on the return trip visited the gold fields on the Kenai Peninsula which in the spring of 1895 was the scene of a minor gold rush on Resurrection and Six Mile Creeks. This strike had lured prospectors from Seattle and other West Coast ports in the early spring of 1896, prior to the big Klondike strike. The first vessel out of Seattle in late February with 27 aboard was lost at sea. The Stella Erland sailed in March with 14 prospectors aboard and was the first to arrive in the Turnagain area, followed by the Bryant and several others including the Utopia, under command of colorful Captain Johnny "Dynamite" O'Brien.

The larger vessels were unable to reach the immediate areas due to ice and the second highest tides in the world, making it necessary to transfer to smaller vessels for landings.

Disappointed on prospects in the area, Jeff sought passage back to Seattle aboard Captain O'Brien's Utopia, which had been chartered to take 100 prospectors and full cargo from Seattle to the Susitna region in Cook Inlet. It was anchored in Seldovia Bay with two other vessels waiting for the to ice clear sufficiently for them to cross the inlet.

Capt. O'Brien had fought for freedom in Ireland, blasting a friend out of prison and had been captured and escaped twice from those attempting to try him for his activities which would have found him sentenced to death. He had narrowly escaped from being eaten by cannibals, fought off pirates in the Pacific almost single handed, had dined with the royal family in the Sandwich Islands (Hawaii), and fallen in love with a Tahitian Princess. He had twice been commended for staying with sinking ships until they could be salvaged.

While in Seldovia Bay this highly regarded sea captain who had earned the moniker of "Dynamite", was stricken with a ruptured tumor.

There was no doctor aboard the Utopia, but one of the crew remembered that there was a miner, a former physician, among those who had come north on the ship.

Luck was with them. The former doctor, going by the name of Crandall, was located in a nearby cabin and after a quick examination "Doc" Crandall explained that it was certain death if he did not operate and a thousand to one chance of O'Brien's recovering if he did. Always a gambler, O'Brien took that one chance.

No instruments for an operation were available other than a butcher knife, a pair of scissors and a needle and spool of thread. Loading Capt. Johnny with whiskey, which was plentiful and also using the spirits to sterilize the "instruments" the operation was completed. After days of hovering between life and death Capt. O'Brien recovered sufficiently to be moved back to the ship and plan on sailing for home.

That however, was not Capt. O'Brien's only problem. Due to delays the ship was out of coal and the plucky Captain had no funds to purchase any.

It was then that a handsome, well built stranger appeared at shipside inquiring about passage to Seattle. Capt. O'Brien, still in intense pain, explained the situation. No money, no coal.

The kindly stranger, who booked passage as Mr. Smith, peeled off five $100 bills, asking if that was sufficient. It was.

Not only that, but Mr. Smith immediately took charge of nursing O'Brien back to health. While the ship was being coaled, Smith cleaned the cabin, obtained the best foods that could be found in the area, prepared it to a chef's delight, and remained at the side of the stricken captain.

In the days prior to the Klondike rush Soapy Smith had one of his most interesting Alaskan experiences on Capt. O'Brien's steamship Utopia. -Seattle Historical Society Photo.

Soon the ship was underway, the vibration of the churning propellers lulling Captain Johnny to the first restful sleep he had enjoyed in ages.

The next thing he remembered was being awaked by the lack of sound or motion from the ships engines. Unable to get up, he tossed a whiskey bottle through the cabin window, attracting the mate's attention.

The mate explained that the crew, under leadership of the chief engineer, had mutinied and refused to continue the journey, claiming that the coal was inferior and that they could not make it back to Seattle under such conditions.

Capt. O'Brien asked that friend Smith be brought to his cabin - having noted that Mr. Smith wore pistols under his coat. The Captain asked to borrow them.

Smith explained that he was not a man of violence, and requested that there be none, but handed the weapons over to O'Brien, and helped the stricken captain to a chair on deck.

O'Brien ordered the chief engineer and engine room crew to file past him and demanded of each that they return to work with the warning that if they did not it would be mutiny as he was still captain of the vessel.

Apparently he was understood. The Utopia crossed the Gulf of Alaska without trouble and refueled at Juneau, with additional funds supplied by Mr. Smith. It then continued to Seattle where a pale Capt. O'Brien made his way ashore on the helpful arm of his friend Smith.

It was not until much later, when their paths crossed in Skagway, that O'Brien learned that his benefactor was none other than the notorious Jefferson Randolph Smith, better known as "Soapy."

Captain O'Brien later related that Smith and some of his men often sailed with him between the Pacific Northwest and Alaska, and that they were always gentlemen aboard his ship and that Smith was always kind-hearted and generous to the crew.

Captain Johnny "Dynamite" O'Brien, one of the most colorful sea captains of the era. He gave Jeff Smith credit for saving his life on the high seas off the coast of Alaska.
- **Clifford Collection.**

31

Following his initial trip, Smith was still interested in the last frontier. He returned to the Pacific Northwest and possibly Denver before heading north again the next year.

Although reports of gold strikes on the upper Yukon River kept making the rounds in various parts of Canada and the United States little attention was paid to them.

In 1896 at the age of 74, Capt. Moore obtained a Dominion Government contract to deliver the Royal Mail from Juneau to Forty Mile, the first such delivery for the Yukon area.

On August 17, 1896 Siwash George Carmack, Tagish Charlie and Skookum Jim (who had served as a guide for Moore on is first trip over the White Pass) discovered gold in Rabbit Creek. The next morning the trio staked their claim to history. Up and down the Yukon prospectors flocked to Bonanza Creek (as Rabbit Creek became known).

The outside world knew little of the strike. At Forty Mile Ogilvie was searching for some means to appraise his government in Ottawa of the situation. Captain Moore had just completed his mail run from Juneau and was heading home. He agreed to carry Ogilvie's brief message along with letters from successful miners who were sending home news of their good fortune. Enroute he passed several stranded parties heading for civilization and helped them along the way, including some who had left 10 days prior to his departure. Ogilvie's message was forwarded to the Canadian government in Ottawa, but nobody paid any attention to it. Ogilvie tried again, without success. Eventually a austere little pamphlet was published but created nary a ripple. Some letters resulted in small items in a few local newspapers.

CHAPTER 9

GOLD. GOLD. GOLD.

All this changed however, when the first of three ships from the North landed in San Francisco, San Diego and Seattle with miners and their pokes of gold.

The Alaska Commerical Co. Excelsior arrived in San Francisco from St. Michael on July 14, 1897 and docked at the foot of Market Street with 25 passengers carrying $189,000 in Klondike gold. The San Francisco newspapers front pages headlines, however, were devoted to the Annie Maud from Calcutta which arrived with bubonic plague aboard. The Excelsior was followed by the S.S. Humboldt putting in at San Diego without any attention at all.

Then on July 17, the Pacific Whaling Co's dirty and battered "Portland" skippered by Captain Kingston arrived in Seattle with 68 miners toting a "Ton of Gold." Worth approximately $700,000 it was unloaded under the watchful eyes of Wells-Fargo Express guards as thousands jammed the Seattle waterfront.

Down the gangplank marched John Wilkerson with $50,000 in gold, Dick McNulty $20,000, Frank Keller $35,000 and Frank Phiscator

Front page of the Seattle Post Intelligencer "Extra" July 17 telling of the arrival of the steamship Portland with its "Ton of Gold." This was the kickoff for the greatest gold rush in history. - Clifford Collection.

staggered ashore under the load of his $96,000. Others had lesser amounts, but all were willing and proud to tell of their experiences, stressing the abundance of gold. This touching off the greatest gold rush in history, thanks in part to the imagination of a former Seattle newspaper editor, Eratus Brainard, employed as a publicity man by the Seattle Chamber of Commerce. He sent out stories worldwide, referring to the "Ton of Gold." The rush was on.

Adding to the mystic was the background of the Portland, the former S.S. Haiti Republic, which had been used to smuggle arms, Chinese coolies and opium to American ports before being seized by the government and sold for use in Alaskan waters. She died an inglorious death a couple of years later when she struck an unseen object and sank in those same Alaskan waters.

In the saloons, on the street corners, wherever idle men gathered, it seemed as if they had been waiting for a miracle to deliver them. Now the sidewalks and wharfs of every Pacific coast port from San Francisco to Vancouver were dotted with groups of excited men conversing with great enthusiasm.

At once a spawn of hucksters sprang up along the waterfront to accommodate the gullible. Peddlers and legitimate traders alike, made fortunes from the sale of useless and shoddy equipment. Klondike supply companies boomed everywhere.

Less innocent diversions were the brothels, saloons and dance halls. Here promoters were particularly adept in milking the men who had money to spend and time to kill. Many were stripped of their cash and pawned their possessions before they could obtain passage to the Klondike. Others remained behind, either beating their way home or disappearing among the legion of missing men.

There were three areas to be worked by the purveyors of pleasure. the dive operators, shills, floosies, bartenders, card sharks and gamblers.

One was the exit ports, where the tenderfoot arrived with wallets full of folding money to buy their outfits and arrange for passage to the North. The second was the entry ports of Alaska where the gold seekers seemed to be in a considerably hurry. The third was the wild towns of the gold frontier, Dawson and the like.

Once clear of the pitfalls of the waterfront, the prospectors still faced the problem of transportation to the Northland. Ticket prices skyrocketed. A flotilla of ships was the weirdest assortment one could imagine. Hulks along the waterfront were pasted together with putty and good intentions to take gold seekers to Alaska and the Klondike. Anything that could float was fitted with tiered bunks, manned with a pickup crew and rushed into service, crammed with five to ten times the number it could hold.

The steamship Queen prior to departing from Seattle with the first gold rush passengers. It was the first vessel to arrive in Skagway in the summer of 1897. Many of the passengers became the hijackers who stole Capt. Billy Moore's property and founded the Committee of One Hundred and One. - Seattle Historical Society.

Within weeks the route from the Seymour Narrows to Lynn Canal was strewn with wreckage of many of the overloaded and poorly manned hulks. Hundreds perished along with countless horses, oxen, dogs and other animals that had been jammed into their leaking and rotting holds.

Passengers were a motley throng. There were those that planned to dig for gold. There were the rich and the poor, clerks, farmers and merchants. intellectuals and illiterates. There were also the parasites, fugitives from justice, gamblers, confidence-men, pimps and prostitutes, proficient in the devious methods of extracting gold from the pokes of their flamboyant victims.

Success stories among the late arrivals were few and fare between. The Mayor of Seattle headed a group which chartered the Humboldt. Most of the Seattle police department joined in. They went via St. Michael and it took them almost a year to get to the Klondike, due to being frozen in the Yukon River during the winter months. They were lucky. Many others were lost.

CHAPTER 10

CAPTAIN MOORE'S LOSING BATTLE

In the early summer of 1897, Skagway had but one family, Captain William Moore's. He had waited 13 years for the Yukon gold rush he was certain would develop. On July 29 his prediction came true. The first gold rush steamer, the Queen skippered by Captain James Carroll, anchored in the bay, and the first hordes of Klondikers piled ashore.

Captain Carroll, unfamiliar with this part of Alaska, remarked to Capt. Moore that they had seen smoke from his cabin and came ashore to ask him a few questions. They wanted to know if they were on the right track to the Klondike and asked about the best place to start from. Moore told them that most went over the Chilkoot trail from nearby Dyea, but he felt that the White Pass trail was a better route. They questioned him as to who owned the land on the bay and Moore informed them that he had owned it for 13 years, but they were welcome to unload their outfits on his small dock and the beach and that he would help them.

Some of the gold seekers camped on the beach for the night. Others returned to the ship. The next morning they started unloading. There were about 200 in the party. Later they held a meeting aboard ship and then informed Moore that they didn't care that he had lived on the property for 13 years, they were taking it over. They jumped his claim and took over his property.

Alaska at the time was ideal for the unlawful. The machinery of the law had not been extended to the territory. From the land of peace and security the trail to the gold fields became a safe field for thugs and outlaws.

Moore, tough old veteran that he was, protested in vain. He was shoved aside. By August 7 there were enough newcomers in Skagway to set up a local, but illegal government and to lay out a town. Dave KcKinney called for a city meeting. One of the most interested was Frank H. Reid, a bartender at the Klondike Saloon, who in the course of his duties acquired a set of survey instruments from a down and out engineer. He immediately became active in the material interests of the community. He was elected "City Engineer" by the provisional but illegal "City Council." He laid out the townsite with 60 foot wide streets and 3600 lots, measuring 50 by 100 feet, which were divided up among the early settlers. The council also changed the name from Mooresville to Skaguay (Skagway), taken from the Indian Skag-waugh, the native term for cruel wind, the icy blast that blew down the canyons from the White Pass.

Argonauts used everything from back packs to horse drawn scows to ferry their possession ashore during the first weeks of the gold rush activity in Skagway. This photo was taken in early August 1897. Tents and a lone building erected by early arrivals can be seen in the background. - Library of Congress.

Reid's survey placed Moore's home in the middle of one of the proposed streets — Broadway. The committee ordered him to move and he angrily refused. They descended on him with peeves and hand spikes. Capt. Moore stood his ground. He grabbed a crowbar and swung at the man nearest him. The crowd broke up, but the Captain knew he had lost the fight and his home was moved to a distant corner of the newly surveyed town.

Members of the committee took possession and sold the lots, 1100 in two days, to new arrivals at high prices, pocketing the funds. Purchasers paid filing fees to U.S. Commissioner J.U. Smith (no relation to Soapy) who had been named recorder. He failed to record the transactions, pocketing the filing fees. Lots were sold over and over again even including an attempt to high-jack and resell the lot purchased for Skagway's first church.

Such actions led to strenuous times. As the original purchasers headed for the Klondike and returning only to find someone else was occupying their property, and if it had been built upon, occupying their cabin. Others found cabins removed from their property. Those who dared leave for only a couple of days were most certain to find the most valuable of buildings — the little one- or two-holer out back had been stolen. Meanwhile Reid wound up owning a one-sixth share of a 39-acre waterfront tract that originally was part of Capt. Moore's homestead.

Moore, meanwhile added to his saw mill and built a dock along the cliffs on the waterfront where the cruise ships land today. He

Map of Skaguay with its lots, streets and alleys as platted by Frank Reid after his survey was approved by the so-called City Council. - Clifford Collection.

became wealthy despite being "robbed" of his original homestead by Reid and the others.

Later Capt. Moore built the largest and most elegant house in Skagway and then leased it to Harriet Pullen, one of the early arrivals. She had worked in a restaurant, baked apple pies at night, ran a pack train and raised her family of kids. Eventually she purchased and turned Moore's house into the finest hotel in the Territory — The Pullen House.

Frank Reid's house in Skagway. - Clifford Collection.

Alexander Pantages, who later founded the Pantages Theater chain, worked for her as a bartender and waiter before heading for the Klondike. President Warren G. Harding spent a night in the Pullen House when he visited Alaska in 1923.

Moore continued his fight in the courts and after the gold rush was over was awarded a settlement of 25 percent of the assessed improvements valued at $100,000 by the United States District Court following the Secretary of Interior in September 1901 ruling in favor of the Moores (Capt. Billy and his son Ben). Capt Moore sold his interest in the wharf for $16,000. He died in March 1909 in Victoria.

Members of the Committee of One Hundred and One moved
Capt. Moore's home from it original claim site to the outskirts of Skagway. Reid deemed its location was in the middle
of Broadway, the main street. Yukon Archives.

By early fall Skagway was divided into two factions — the skinned
and the skinners. The skinners were better organized and stuck together,
so that those who were defrauded were unable to obtain redress.

The town of Skagway, conceived in anarchy and lawlessness, was
founded on stolen property and grew up on violence.

Once the invasion began, the region between Lynn Canal and
the Canadian border atop the coastal mountains became the resort of
criminals. A month passed before Uncle Sam, who had not anticipated
a rush of such magnitude, made any pretense at establishing law.

By August a commissioner and a deputy United States marshal
had been appointed to protect private rights and property and a company of U.S. Army troops were stationed in Dyea and Skagway. The
new officials, however, were not vested with powers to deal with pecu-
liar local conditions, nor could the soldiers be called upon unless martial law was proclaimed.

To indemnify the authorities against wasting public funds on
frivolous, unfounded allegations, aggregated parties had to lodge formal complaints before the commissioner and enter into written recog-
nizance guaranteeing their attendance at a trial, with defaulters liable
to a stiff penalty. These provisions assisted the evil-doers by working
to the disadvantage of the victim, and made the law ridiculous in the
eyes of both. A transient, naive enough to evoke their terms, either

waited at Dyea or Skagway pending the arrest of the offender, or ran the risk of being called back from the trail — an alternative which might entail the disastrous abandonment, until his return, of an irreplaceable outfit strewn perhaps for miles in the bush.

In short, the cure was worse than the disease. Rather than submit to it, a man who had been cheated, robbed or beaten, bore his wrong in silence.

For the first five months of the rush, or until the passes closed during the winter of 1896-97, the NWMP's did not require a set amount of food or equipment, but after the near starving in Dawson that winter they required roughly enough foodstuff for a year plus other equipment, making for a ton or more that each prospector had to transport from Skagway to Dawson, one way or another.

Also, there was a 25 to 30 percent duty on all goods purchased in the U.S. and taken into Canada.

The White Pass closed in September 1897 when Lake Bennett froze up and reopened May 29, 1898 when the ice broke up on the lake and the rush of the thousands who had wintered at Lake Bennett and in Skagway was on.

NWMP figures indicated that more than 60,000 persons went over Chilkoot and White Pass during the first two years of the rush. This was the Skagway and the situation that was to greet Soapy and his followers when they arrived.

CHAPTER 11
RETURN TO ALASKA

On his second trip to Alaska Soapy was accompanied by "Reverend" John Bowers, George Wilder, Syd Dixon, "Slim Jim" Foster and Van Triplett, known as "Old Man" Tripp. Bowers was closest to Soapy and a sort of "right hand man." His saintly appearance, gentle voice and benevolent mien inspired confidence. He was the best "bunco-steerer" in the profession, a "glad hander" who knew the grips and signals of every lodge and fraternal order. Spotting a lodge emblem on the lapel or the ring on the finger of a prospect, he would warmly embrace his victim in the spirit of brotherhood and the "fraternal brother" became clay in the potter's hands.

Wilder excruded an atmosphere of prosperity and well being. He was the "successful businessman." He was dexterous with figures and an authority on investment opportunities and could direct an affluent prospect into a "sure thing." He was the advance man for the gang and also the only member of the group with enough ready cash to finance the Alaska trip. He was a godsend to Soapy in this respect.

Dixon was a "shill." Unlike his colleagues, he lacked the dedication to the role he had to play. He came from a wealthy family and was a world traveler addicted to opium. His role as a shill and his acquaintance to the con-games provided him with money sufficient to meet the demands of his addiction.

Foster was another shill. His pose was that of an inexperienced tenderfoot and his naivete and disarming manner soon won the confidence of his unwitting prospect as strangers warmed up to him.

Tripp was the opposite number of Foster. He posed as an experienced prospector, a sourdough hardened by the fires of the frontier. His weathered face, framed by his long white hair and sage advice so thoroughly given to the cheechakos, or greenhorns, on the trail, effectively masked the cold-blooded scoundrel that he was.

The first stop was Wrangell which was ready for the Klondike onslaught via the "All-Canadian" route up the Stikine River to Glenora and Telegraph Creek via steamboat, then by trail to Lake Teslin where connections were made with river steamers for the trip down the Yukon.

Much remained from the earlier Cassiar rush of 1884 which found gamblers and ladies of leisure coming up from Victoria. The roulette wheels whirled and the dance halls flourished, ably handled by such as Dick Willoughby and "Dancing Bill" Latham.

The first few weeks of August saw at least 10 ships unloading prospectors in the Wrangell area. Local riverboats carried the prospectors up river and return.

Wrangell at about the time Soapy Smith stopped off on this second Alaska visit. One writer described it as "the most tumble-down looking company of cabins I ever saw." Hegg Photo.

Juneau was a well organized community when Jeff and his cohorts stopped of there briefly following his visit to Wrangell. - Clifford Collection.

One occasion after a very productive trip, the purser of one such boat was carrying proceeds from the trip to the company headquarters when he was held up and relieved of several thousand dollars in cash.

Walking in town the next morning the purser ran into Soapy Smith and accused him of allowing his men to stage the robbery, commenting that there should be honor among them in that the riverboats were bringing in the suckers for Soapy and his men to trim. In so doing they should be immune to actions of the gang.

Soapy remarked that such had not previously been called to his attention and that he would look into it. He remarked that he was not certain that it was his men that staged the robbery. In parting he stated that he would try to find out just what had happened and suggested that the purser drop by his place that evening.

The young purser called at Soapy's office and was happily surprised when Smith returned the money, with the remark that he guessed that the boy was right, "there should be honor among thieves," indicating that the rates the ships charged passengers and freight haulers was "robbery" of the first degree.

Although Soapy and his cohorts were successful in their forays in Wrangell it was not to his liking. Wyatt Earp, who visited Wrangell shortly after Soapy, described it as "hell on wheels filled with con men, gun men, prostitutes, ne'er do-wells and gamblers, all of whom had come to make their fortunes by taking advantage of prospectors straight from the gold fields.

Wrangell's Klondike rush was short lived as the Canadian government refused to give land grants in consideration on of the building of a railroad from Telegraph Creek to Teslin.

Smith and his followers moved on the Juneau, which had been a mining camp since 1880 when Richard Harris and Joe Juneau discovered gold in Gold Creek. Miner's law prevailed from Feb 1881 until July 1884. By 1883 Juneau had become a stable town of some 1,500 residents. It was the mining center of Alaska, with the rich Treadwell claims on Douglas Island owned by San Francisco interests. In 1900 Juneau was named capital of the Territory, replacing Sitka which had been the Russian capital. By 1906 U.S. government offices had been moved into Juneau. The town was not to Soapy's liking so he moved on to the Indian village of Dyea.

The tent city was the jumping off place for the treacherous trail over the Chikoot Pass. The town was throbbing with activity, containing all the ingredients that Soapy was seeking. It was the right size and age to exploit. There was no constitutional government, only a federal marshal's office and a company of American soldiers who were kept busy patrolling the trail and reminding the North West Mounted Police that this was American, not Canadian territory.

The Healy and Wilson trading post in Dyea, founded in 1885-86, along with two saloons were the center of activities at the time Soapy Smith and his followers landed prior to settling in Skagway. Little other than a few wharf posts remain today. - Yukon Archives.

To the multitude, Soapy presented a striking figure. Black-bearded, well groomed, slender and of good physique, Jefferson R. Smith carried himself with an air of quiet authority. This was also virgin territory for his skilled henchmen. They took over the town and within hours of landing had their games operating and money was pouring in.

Marshal James Shoup was out of town, having taken some prisoners to Sitka and had left his nephew, John W. Shoup, a newly sworn in deputy, in charge.

It was not long before a heated argument broke out in a saloon between an angry young man who had lost considerable in a shell game with one of Soap's crew. The tall, slender and alert deputy was soon on hand. He listened to both sides of the argument, ordered the money returned to the victim and took the shells.

Shortly thereafter Soapy was sitting across the desk from the deputy, pleading the case of his cohort, with the explanation that the young man who lost his money was just a transient passing through, soon to be on his way spending little money in town.

By contrast, Smith explained, he and his friends intended to stay in town and provide entertainment for the transient prospectors, spend their money with local merchants, and in addition he would make it very much worthwhile for the marshal and his deputy.

The reception was a cool one. The deputy explained that Marshal Shoup would be returning in the morning and suggested that Smith and his friends leave town prior to his arrival if they wanted to avoid real trouble. He then ordered Soapy out of the office.

In the meantime, Soapy had send Reverend Bowers on an exploratory visit to Skagway, some six miles down the coast.

Bowers brought back a glowing report of a wide-open tent city that was ripe for picking. Also, in contrast to the Chilkoot Pass, the White Pass would not be open during the winter months and a backup of men would build up at the gateway.

In view of the deputy marshal's edict it seemed wise to vacate Dyea in favor of the potential of Skagway.

Within 24 hours of their arrival in Skagway Jeff's henchmen were manipulating their walnut shells, pitting their wits against all comers, and running their confidence games while Soapy was orienting himself as he moved through the crowds.

CHAPTER 12
JEFF'S PLACE

Shortly after arriving in Skagway Jeff went into partnership with John Clancy, a respected owner of a small saloon on the outskirts of town. A short time later they acquired the small 15 by 50 foot former First Bank of Skagway building on Holly St. and named it Jeff Smith's Parlors (Parlor), featuring choice wines and liquors and an oyster bar.

During their partnership, Clancy acquired other properties on his own and in cooperation with Frank Clancy, resulting in many believing Soapy was involved in such. This was not the case as noted on his death less than a year later Smith's estate consisted mainly of half interest in the Holly St. property.

This very modest saloon at 317 Holly St. had a bar, a small card alcove and a door that led from the bar into a store room and a small back yard. There was also a small room with a desk, which was Smith's office. There was no evidence of gambling equipment other than cards. Over the years, the tiny saloon building, twice moved and now located on the waterfront near where Smith and Reid met in their fatal shootout, grew to giant proportions if one is to believe the many

John Clancy's original saloon prior to his going into partnership with Soapy Smith. This photo was taken a few weeks after the first argonauts landed in Skagway. Smith and Clancy later took over the First Bank of Skagway building on Holly St. (Sixth Ave.).- Clifford Collection.

Jeff Smith (with white hat) and some of his followers in front of Jeff Smith's Parlor (also known as Parlors)s. - Clifford Collection.

articles written about the King of Skagway. A few examples:

"His (Soapy's) saloon and gambling establishment in Skagway was one of he most elaborate the northwest ever saw. It had one rival for size and none for ferocity or double dealing," was the description in a magazine article first published in St. Louis and then Denver, quoting an alleged "eye witness" to the shootout on the wharf.

In 1920 the same article appeared in the Literary Digest, one of the most respected publications of that era.

Historian Don Steffa's, Tales of Noted Frontier Characters - Soapy Smith, Bad Man And Bluffer, in Pacific Monthly of October 1908, described Jeff's Place.

"After clearing thousands through his gambling privilege (supposedly in a large wholesale liquor house), Soapy closed shop again and within a few days opened Jeff's Place, a combination saloon, restaurant and gambling den, on Holly street. The robberies and other crimes committed within the walls of the place are beyond adequate description. Soapy watched the operation with a criminal keenness and promptitude that prevented anything but a plethoric condition of the exchequer."

Scarlet & Gold, official NWMP publication, stated that of the 70 or so saloons in Skagway at the time none compared to Soapy's "on so lavish a scale as his own." Jeff's Place (as it was sometimes called) had

Advertisement for Jeff Smith's Parlors which appeared in several Skagway publications. - Clifford Collection.

a capacious gaming room containing crap tables, roulette and faro paraphernalia, wheels of fortune, keno, the Klondike game vingl-et-un and gambling devices of every kind. Half a dozen or more varieties of poker were conducted by unemotional visored dealers. One end of the establishment was occupied by a 44-inch wide polished hardwood bar -an ornate affair, reflected in frosted mirrors — along which white coated Nate Pollock dexterously tossed the drinks to the clientele.

"Soapy's local wolf pack was supplemented by ladies of easy virtue, working on commission, whose task it was to encourage prodigality among the customers"

In his biography of Klondike Mike Mahoney, Merrill Denison describes Smith's facility as a combination saloon, dance hall and gambling parlour with the dance floor having a five-piece orchestra and with white coated waiters almost as plentiful as customers in the crowded facility. Everywhere opulent touches reflected the success of Soapy and his partner John Clancy. There was a polished hardwood bar with frosted mirrors, artificial palm trees flanking the raised stage and fretwork screening above the private boxes."

He also mentioned that Mahoney was offered a lucrative job by Soapy after having brought $125,000 in gold safely from the Klondike via dog sled for the Northern Commercial Co. Klondike Mike also took time out to thoroughly thrash the roughest and toughest bouncer in Skagway. The latter could well be true as Mike later went to Nome where he bested professional boxer Tommy Burns in a match some

Skagwayites line up in front of Dr. Harry Runnalls' Drug Store to receive their mail. Dr. Runnalls handled the mail on volunteer basis when the U.S. Government neglected to do so. He charged a nickel a letter, for both incoming and outgoing mail as no postage stamps were available in Skagway. Later, when the U.S. Government took over the mail service, residents stated that Dr. Runnells had done a better job. - Clifford Collection.

months before Burns defeated James J. Jefferies for the world's heavyweight championship. Mahoney came out of the gold country rich enough that he turned down a lucrative offer for a championship bout with Burns.

Harold Merritt Stumer in This Was Klondike Fever writes, "— in the fall of 1897 Soapy built an enormous saloon, dance hall and gambling hall which he called Jeff's Place and staffed it with his crew of able helpers."

Another who claimed to have arrived in Skagway on August 1, 1897 who wrote and lectured on the early days of the gold rush was C.T. Albrecht. He stated that "Soapy Smith had no saloon and there was no eagle at the back end of the lot. His main hangout was at George Rice's Saloon."

Such were the descriptions of Jeff's Parlors, sitting comfortably on half a standard lot (25 feet) as surveyed by Frank Reid.

This was not always the case. In Denver Soapy had the Tivoli Saloon and Gambling Hall at the corner of 17th and Market Sts. It had large gambling rooms on the second floor. Soapy had only two rules

Union Church, Skagway's first. Jeff Smith was a large contributor to the church fund drive conducted by the Rev. Robert Dickey. Dedicated on December 12, 1897, it was open to all denominations and also served as Skagway's first school. Although in Skagway less than six months, Rev. Dickey also was a key factor in building the town's first hospital, to which Smith was also a major contributor. - Clifford Collection.

for employees. Keep the people from Denver out (Soapy never knowingly cheated locals), and never let an outsider leave if he still had money in his pocket. The Tivoli was one of Denver's most profitable clubs. realizing how it operated Jeff's legal aides advised him to put up a disclaimer near the head of the stairway bearing the words CAVEAT EMPTOR. It meant "Let the Buyer Beware." in Latin. Few, if any, of Soapy's customers read Latin, but it stood him well should there be complain about losing a big sum at the Tivoli.

One such occasion saw two real estate brokers, their pockets crammed with the proceeds from a recently closed, but questionable deal in California, sauntered into the Tivoli with thoughts of adding some easy money to their gains. Six hours later they stormed out, relieved of every penny. The two immediately went to the police and swore out a warrant for Soapy's arrest on a charge of operating rigged games. Hauled before a panel of magistrates Soapy presented his defense in masterful style. Calling attention to his disclaimer, he declared that at the Tivoli no one was compelled to play the games and no one was discouraged from playing. "We let experience be the teacher," Soapy declared. "No player can win at my games and when a man goes broke at one of my tables he'd learned a lesson that he will never forget. I am therefore providing a valuable and moral community service by operating the Tivoli."

Case dismissed.

Almost as elaborate was the Orleans Club in Creede, which Soapy shared with his close companion Joe Simons. It compared favorable with saloons operated by Bat Masterson and Bob Ford. Although it was very successful Soapy sold the Orleans Club for a song when he decided to return to Denver after Simon's death.

Goings on in some of the other Skagway night spots made Jeff's Parlors tame by comparison. In one of the so-called legitimate variety theaters Joe Brooks, a young man engaged in hauling freight over the White Pass, paid $750 for a box of cigars and $3,000 for drink in a single evening. The clip joint proprietor even had the gall to complain to Col. Sam Steele of the North West Mounted Police that the freighter still owed $1,000 for the night's fun. Steele refused to collect the sum and also warned the owner to stay on the American side of the border.

The Canadians on March 27, 1898 had installed a Yukon Commission and North West Mounted Police staff in Skagway and they remained until May 11, when they moved up to Lake Bennett, some 25 miles into recognized Canadian territory.

There was no postoffice in Skagway at the time, so by common consent Dr. H.B Runnells, a dentist, collected the mail off incoming ships and deposited letters on outbound vessels for which he received 5 cents per letter. Postage stamps were non existent in Skagway.

Early in his Skagway stay, Soapy realized a big need of the greenhorns was to get information to and from the folks back home. As a result Soapy set up a telegraph office ballyhooed by a sign over the door reading. "Wires to Anywhere in the United States." Messages were dutifully taken and a $5 fee charged for the service. After a reasonable time, replies could be had on a "collect" basis.

Many of the answers requested funds to take care of an emergency at home. Any amount could be handled through Soapy's telegraph office at a cost of $5 plus the amount to be sent.

The telegraph office was extremely popular. The fact that there was no telegraph wires into Skagway at the time did not disturb the telegraphers in the least. The end of the outgoing line from the office was buried a few feet from the building. The funds got no further than Soapy's pocket.

Such remained so for many months, until John Clum, formerly of Tombstone and who became a government postal representative, approved of a government postoffice in Skagway.

In addition Jeff started several other businesses such as a Merchant's Exchange, Cut Rate Ticket Office and Reliable Packers. All were tuned to extract as much money as possible from the newcomers and to learn as much as possible about an argonaut's finances, where he kept his funds, his interests and the best way to get him into the clutches of Soapy's followers.

While Smith waited for the right opportunity before making his big move to endear himself to the business community he performed another of his good deeds. A distraught father, a prominent Seattle businessman, came to Skagway in search of his runaway daughter.

Learning of the situation, Smith was all ears as the father related that she had skipped out with a tinhorn and that he had learned that she was working in a Skagway dancehall and turning over all her earnings to the man.

As was his wont, Smith was prompt in his investigation and in no time at all learned that the girl, only 17 years of age, had been induced by her companion to leave home under the promise of marriage. No marriage took place and the report that her lover had placed her in a dance hall proved to be true.

Smith ordered the pair be brought to him.

The girl, hysterical and tearful, rushed to her father and begged to be taken home, but the man, a no-good wastrel, was defiant and insisted that the girl had come north with him willingly and added "it was nobody's business what he did."

Smith took exception and warned that there was no place in Skagway for such and ordered a couple of his newly found followers to take the young man outside and give him the works. He then made arrangements for space on a ship sailing within an hour for the most appreciative father and daughter to return to Seattle. He personally escorted them to the wharf.

Upon his return he faced the bedraggled, badly bruised and thoroughly frightened young ruffian and curtly and coldly gave him instructions to be out of town before nightfall and never to return to Skagway.

CHAPTER 13
BRAWL IN SEATTLE

As fall rolled around Smith and his cohorts had things in Skagway well enough put together that when he received word that his wife in St. Louis was ill, he was able to leave Skagway in mid-September to visit her.

This despite the fact that Jack Jolly, a gang leader recently released from the Montana State penitentiary after serving time on a manslaughter charge, had like Soapy, brought some of his followers to Skagway with hopes of gaining control of the community.

Jolly remarked that "Skagway was the easiest graft in the country," and that he intended to winter there with his followers.

Soapy is said to have met Jolly in Butte, Mont. and apparently was not impressed. There was the story that Smith shot and killed Jolly as a result of a card game in Butte, but there is no record of such. Instead the city records show that in 1882 Jolly was on the city payroll as both town marshal or policeman as well a deputy fireman.

It was also in Butte that Molly Demruska abdicated as queen of the local Cyprians to wed Jolly. After the ceremony in the Clipper Shades Saloon where Soapy is said to have shot Jolly, the couple paraded about town on the city's fire engine. Though the wedding withdrew Molly from the ranks of the ribaldry, admirers delighted in referring to her as Jolly Molly.

Jolly, not too successful in Skagway, later went on to Nome where exaggerations in law enforcement compared with the high level of infamy reached by crooks. In 1903 Police Chief John J. Jolly shot his deputy Sam James following an argument on Front Street.

Jolly was arrested and the prosecution claimed the shooting was a result of falling out between thieves. Jolly was successful in his trial when a key witness came to his defense. Nome had had enough. Jolly did not get his law enforcement job back.

Another Skagway gang, to which Smith paid little attention, was the O'Leary bunch which survived Smith's demise and also moved on to Nome, where there was no Soapy to keep things in order.

It was ironical that as Smith left Skagway on Sept. 14 on the Queen Wyatt Earp, lawman and gunfighter, headed for Alaska on Sept. 23 aboard the Roaslie after a layover of more than three weeks in San Francisco as a result of an injury.

If it had not been for Wyatt's injuring in all probability he would have been a member of Soapy Smith's "staff". Instead both were enroute in different directions between Skagway and Seattle.

Earp arrived in Wrangell, where Soapy had spent a short time before moving to Dyea and Skagway. Upon learning of Smith's absence and the fact that his wife Josie was pregnant, Wyatt decided to head back to Seattle and San Francisco instead of staying in Alaska. He was offered the post of deputy marshal in Wrangell but turned it down although he filled in for 10 days while awaiting a south bound ship. There is evidence that Wyatt was interested in serving in a law enforcing program with Soapy, much like Smith had set up in Denver and Creede.

Wyatt returned to Alaska after Smith's death with stops in Rampart and St. Michael before settling down as a saloon keeper in Nome.

Enroute back to Skagway from St. Louis, Jeff stopped off in Seattle to visit friends. Apparently he had in mind the securing of a law enforcement officer for Skagway. It was a favorite ploy of his in taking over a community to bring in a respected police authority to maintain order. Such had been the case in Creede where he brought in Captain John Light. He also made certain that prominent businessmen were named mayor and aldermen. It was by this method that Smith established a government which would not interfere with his own activities but at the same time would insure peace in the community and provide

Entryway to the former Horseshoe Saloon at 614 First Ave. on Seattle's Pioneer Square. It was here that Soapy tangled with some of the city's ruffians. The general thought was that the fight was started in an effort to make certain that Soapy did not set up shop in Seattle. - H. Clifford.

efficient regulation with ample protection for it residents, providing municipal control which was efficient and yet enabled everyone to have a good time. To no small degree, he succeeded.

By this time Seattle had surpassed San Francisco's Barbary Coast as the "wickedest city in America." Its tenderloin featured interesting and notorious "box houses", a combination of the more desirable features of saloons, burlesque theaters, dance halls and brothels. They had come under control of John Considine and the likes of John Pennell despite occasional reform movements.

Big gambling houses like the Totem, the Dawson and the Union were operating 24 hours a day as were the glittering parlor houses, one of which advertised as the world's largest, another claimed to have girls of every race and nationality, and Madam Kate's where the girls were driven to work by livery retainers, no profanity was allowed, and free medical attention was guaranteed any gentleman who could prove he had come to grief in that refined establishment.

Considine reopened the Peoples Theater as a box house with the notorious Little Egypt as the star attraction. He took over Billy The Mug's Saloon at 2nd and Washington with the Owl Club Rooms above.

During his Seattle stopover Smith visited with friends, such as Jimmy Dugan, a former Denver law officer now well established in Seattle.

On the evening of October 1, 1897 Soapy and Dugan decided to take a look around and wound up in the Horseshoe Saloon at 614 1st Ave. just off Yesler, in what is now Pioneer Square. It wasn't long before Elmer Mayberry, a well known Seattle sporting man spotted Smith and they soon came to words, tossed glasses and spittoons, and then threw punches with Smith, much smaller and lighter than Mayberry, getting the worse of it. Dugan joined in to protect his friend Smith and soon Eddie Gaffney, a professional athletes and strong arm man for some of the local gamblers, entered in the fracas. Within minutes the four had trashed the interior of the Horseshoe, including one of the glass doors.

Order was not restored until another local sporting man, Jack Thompson entered and drew a gun, putting an end to the action. During the fight, Smith and Dugan suffered bruises, Mayberry received a stab wound which required medical attention and Gaffney found his jacket ripped to shreds.

By the time police arrived, Mayberry, Gaffney and Thompson had left. Smith and Dugan remained. As Mayberry refused to file a complaint, Detectives Cudihee and Meredith did not make any arrests. They made it clear, however, that Smith was not welcome to stay in Seattle. Word around the Tenderloin was to the effect that the fracas was staged as a warning to Smith that he was not welcome to operate in Seattle.

After the Horseshoe affair Smith met with Willie Loomis, a former Leadville police chief and attempted to entice Loomis to return to Skagway with him. Soapy stated, "I'm going to be boss of Skagway. I know just how I'm going to do it and if you come along, I'll make you chief of police."

Loomis declined and tried to talk Soapy out of returning to Skagway, convinced that it would be his doom.

About the same time that Soapy returned to Skagway, a 25-year old Presbyterian minister, the Rev. Robert McCohan Dickey arrived in Skagway on Friday, Oct. 7 1897. He started a Union Church building campaign on Oct. 21, 1897.

Needless to say, Smith helped push the campaign to construct Skagway's first church, making a heavy contribution from his winnings at Faro in the Pack Train Inn. The old oft told story originating in Creede that he kept a check on donations for the good of the pastor, and then had one of his boys steal the kitty when it was fat enough, is a bit too preposterous at this time. No records show such nor had any of those active in the church fund drive made such a remark.

Instead some of the early arrivals who became the Committee of 101 attempted to high-jack the church lot and "resell" it before the church was built. It was completed in record time and although Soapy was visiting his family in St. Louis for the Christmas holidays when the church was dedicated several of his more trustworthy followers were in attendance, and made heavy donations in the collection plate.

It was not until after it had been installed that Rev. Dickey learned that the "church" bell, sold to him by a couple of "prospectors" had been stolen from a ship in the harbor. When he tried to return the bell the captain made it a donation to the community. The church also served as Skagway's first school as well as a Sunday school and it was open for use by all denominations.

The story is told, whether it is true or not, that when the Right Reverend Peter Trimble Rowe, the pioneer Bishop of Alaska, was robbed on the trail out of Skagway by one of the local ruffians, the miscreant, on learning his victim's identity handed back the pouch of gold.

"Why do you give this back?" Rowe asked in astonishment. "

Hell, Bishop," replied the thief, "I'm a member of your congregation."

CHAPTER 14

STORM AT SEA

On one of his trips between the Pacific Northwest and Alaska Smith endeared himself with the sea captains as he showed himself on the side of constituted authority and prevented bloodshed aboard ship It was in early January 1898 after having spent Christmas in St. Louis with his family.

Soapy was aboard the City of Seattle, one of the typical hell ships plying the route — over crowded, poor quarters, worse food, improper facilities and inadequate and sometimes dangerous equipment.

Two of the passengers, apparently having had too much to drink,were climbing and roughhousing in the rigging, swinging from the ropes. One of them loosened a heavy lamp which hit him on the head, killing him instantly.

The disgruntled and rowdy passengers who had witnessed the incident, met to decide whether to take over the ship, sue the captain and crew or take other dangerous actions. Sensing a possibly riot Jeff Smith asked if anyone knew the dead person. None responded. He then asked for someone to search the man for identification. No one wanted to touch the dead man so Soapy pretended to search him for some identification. In so doing he came up with his own wallet and loudly proclaimed that the dead man, a stowaway who had asked of Soapy

The steamship City of Seattle at the Moore Dock in Skagway. It was on this vessel that Soapy Smith prevented a possible riot after one of the passengers was killed while swinging through the ship's superstructure. - Clifford Collection.

permission to sleep in his cabin, had stolen from him.

Holding the "stolen" wallet aloft, Jeff called the victim a thief, a cheat and a bum and asked the crowd in his most persuasive manner if they were willing to throw the ship into such turmoil over such a person.

As was his custom, he swayed the crowd and pursuability an innocent but unknown man was buried at sea under the stigma of a thief, but it averted the possible shedding of blood. This made Smith valuable friends among ship captains and crews, especially Capt. Hunter and Purser T. Pope of the City of Seattle.

Although Smith was friendly with most of the sea captains who brought their ships to Skagway, he was also partial to the working man — most of whom probably gambled at one time or another.

Labor trouble rose in Skagway when the Pacific Coast Steamship Co. cut the wages from 75 cents to 50 cents an hour for those workers unloading ships. Then the shipping company brought a gang of Indians aboard from Juneau, willing to work for 25 cents an hour.

This infuriated the Skagway men, many of whom were would-be Klondikers without funds and who were desperately in need of work. A pitched battle ensued at the sight of Indians doing the job that they had come down to the dock to do. The Skagway workers banished the Indians from the dock, chasing them back on the ship. This resulted in the Captain threatening to have the Mate turn a scalding hot water hose on those on the dock unless they left.

Such was not to be, however. Jeff Smith appeared with a gun and threatened to shoot the Mate if he turned on the water. He then sat down and negotiated with the Captain an arrangement whereby the Skagway crew would work on the docks and the Indians aboard the ship. Thus peace was restored and Soapy Smith was the peacemaker once again.

CHAPTER 15
REID AND THE OTHER SMITH

Frank H. Reid was among the first gold seekers to land at Skagway, arriving in late July or early August 1897. After finishing college in Michigan, Frank and his older brother Dick, had headed for Oregon in 1873 where they taught school. Frank, however, did not care for that lifestyle and became a surveyor, construction worker and volunteer "Indian fighter" with Mart Brown's company of Oregon Volunteers. This was during the Bannock-Piute War of 1878 in Eastern Oregon. It is said he was among those accused of inciting some of the Indians to fight the settlers in order to keep the volunteers busy.

In November 1879 Reid was charged in Sweet Home, Ore. with the murder of an unarmed man who refused to speak to him when Reid requested he do so. Reid pleaded self defense and in January 1880 a jury found him not guilty.

Reid, however, found it healthier to move elsewhere, including Whatcom (now Bellingham) in Washington where he was a surveyor. It is very possible that he and Smith had crossed paths in Western Oregon as Jeff was in the same general area during part of that period and is known to have met some of Dick Reid's relatives.

In as much as the pioneer Oregonians made their own soap Smith confined his activities in Oregon to the walnut and pea routine, which caught the eye of the "country bumpkins" who thought they could put one over on the "city slicker."

Smith and Reid appeared cordial to each other in Skagway although their philosophies differed. They often found time to have a couple of drinks together when they met on the street.

Smith was of the opinion that there should be law and order under control of the proper police officers who would perhaps turn the other way as far as gambling (which was legal at the time) and other games were concerned, but would draw the line on violence and bloodshed. This was the case in Creede where Smith kept crime, in the meaning of the word at that time, under control and barred ruffians and cutthroats.

On the other hand, Reid firmly believed that when law enforcement broke down or officers failed to or were unwilling to enforce the law it was the duty for citizens to take the law into their own hands.

Except for that point the two got along well and respected each other. Reid always referred to Smith as "Jeff", never Soapy.

One day while chatting at the bar, Smith commented, "Frank, there is only one man in Alaska who can get me. If I am ever got, you'll be the man who'll do it."

Frank H. Reid, was a hero to many. To others he was a villain, having murdered an unarmed man in Oregon and was one of the leaders of the Committee of One Hundred and One (Vigilantes) who hijacked Captain Billy Moore's property to set up the town of Skagway. - Clifford Collection.

"I know it, Jeff," was Reid's only comment.

Jeff Smith was not the only Smith in Skagway to create disdain for American law enforcement. The other was U.S. Commissioner John U. Smith, (no relation). However, many newspaper accounts and word of mouth reports of lawlessness in Skagway did not differentiate between the two Smiths (the first initial being the same) with Soapy getting the blame for everything in as much as the other Smith had been appointed by the federal government in July 1897. He also served as recorder for the so called Skagway township, accepting recording fees on the sale of property, but failing to register such.

When things began to get hot for Commissioner Smith he decided to show his superiors that he was attempting to run a respectable town. He and his Marshal decided to stop all gambling and close all sporting houses in Skagway. This, however, resulted in all such operations paying a $25 fine for violations and continuing business as usual. Comm. Smith and the Marshal divided the funds, and there was no record of such fines on the city's books.

Comm. Smith tried a man who had committed an assault in his presence. He agreed to reduce the charge from attempted murder - a felony which would be tried in the district court in Sitka - to assault and battery for which the fine and fees totaled $150 (which Smith could pocket). Contrary to Smith's expectations, the accused man did not think the reduced charge in exchange for $150 was a good deal and insisted that he be tried in district court.

Not only that. The Commissioner visited Haines, an Indian village 16 miles southwest of Skagway, and collected $400 in recording fees for town lots the Indians had long occupied. He also gouged high recorder fees in the all-important transactions of filing on mining claims, and assessed exorbitant court costs at hearings. Acting as an attorney he was accused of charging high fees for defending clients in a private capacity in district court. It was pointed out that at times deputy marshals and commissioners under such circumstances worked together to make business by stirring up strife and contentions to get fees. Things got so bad in Skagway that Gov. John Brady had the federal government remove Commissioner Smith from office in March 1898.

CHAPTER 16
SOAPY'S TAKES OVER

Soapy's big chance came on January 24, 1898 shortly after his return from a Christmas visit home. A Deputy U.S. Marshal and a saloon patron were shot and killed by a bartender.

The shooting took place when Andy McGrath, a worker on the Brackett toll road, ordered a drink in the Palace Theater Saloon. John E. Fay, the bartender, served McGrath. The customer tendered a dollar for the drink and did not receive any change, as was the custom in Skagway at the time. The two got into an argument. Fay ordered McGrath out of the saloon, with the latter promising to "come back and take care of things."

McGrath went in search of Deputy U.S. Marshal John Rowan and attempted to borrow his revolver "to settle a little matter." So insistent was McGrath that Marshal Rowan agreed to accompany him in an attempt to settle the dispute, despite the fact that at the time Rowan was seeking a doctor to tend his wife who was about to give birth to a child.

Upon entering the saloon, they were met by a blast from Fay's pistol, McGrath was killed instantly and Rowan mortally wounded. He was taken to the office of Dr. J.J. Moore who was at the hospital delivering the Rowan youngster (the first child to be born in Skagway) and then rushed back to his office to tend Marshal Rowan.

Angry citizens took Fay into custody. Having obtained a rope from a nearby hardware store they were in the process of stringing him up on a nearby tree. Smith heard the commotion, grabbed his Winchester rifle and with some of his followers went into action.

He rushed through the crowd, knocked down the man with the rope as his followers grabbed Fay and surrounded him. Calm and unperturbed Smith threatened to put a bullet through the head of anyone who attempted to put a rope around Fay's neck.

"Lynching doesn't go here," Soapy shouted. "How do you know this man deserves to hang? We will let the law take its course and I personally will see that Fay gets a fair trial."

This calmed down some of the more sober members of the mob and when Soapy's men threatened those who did not agree, Smith took command.

Soapy openly questioned Fay and in explaining what had happened declared that he felt his life was in danger and shot in self defense.

Smith then convinced the crowd that Fay should have a fair trial, and pointed out that if the crowd tried to lynch Fay, there would be a wholesale slaughter.

Soapy Smith's saloon draped in black marking the 100th anniversary of his shootout with Frank Reid on July 8, 1998. - Clifford Collection.

Smith's men escorted Fay to jail. With feelings running high there was fear that the crowd might make another attempt to lynch Fay. Smith secretly had him moved to a private home where his followers stood guard.

The next morning a meeting was held in the Union Church with Major John F.A.Strom, editor of the Skagway News and later Territorial Governor, named chairman and attorney Samuel Lovell, secretary. Two committees were appointed, one to investigate the shooting and another to guard the prisoner, who Smith had turned over to T.M. Ward, a much respected citizen. It was also decided that a trial would be held the next day.

In the meantime U.S. Marshal James Shoup from Dyea returned to Skagway, arrested Fay and immediately transported him to Sitka. Shortly thereafter Marshal Shoup named S.S. Taylor as Deputy Marshal for the Skagway area, replacing Rowan. In a trial some time later Fay was found not guilty on the basis of self defense.

Upon learning that Mrs. Rowan had given birth to a youngster at the time Marshal Rowan was shot, Soapy immediately started a collection for her, heading the list himself with a donation of $50. He collected an estimated $2,000 which was turned over to her. Later Soapy joined forces with others in taking up another collection which was divided between Mrs. McGrath and Mrs. Rowan.

The Reverend J. A. Sinclair, Presbyterian minister, who arrived in Skagway at about the time of the Fay affair was surprised with the goings on. He wrote his wife in reference to the meeting in the church.

"A lynching bee held in a church," he wrote," and the Robin Hood of the town controlled the meeting and practically nominated the committee and with the desperado at the same time protecting the murderer and taking up a public subscription for the widow of his victim."

It was during this period that Col. Sam Steele of North West Mounted Police passed through Skagway to take over command in the Yukon and remarked that "it was little better than hell on earth," the roughest place in the world. Robbery and murder occurred daily. Shots were exchanged on the streets in broad daylight. At night the clash of bands and the shouts of "murder" mingled with the cracked voices of singers in the variety halls.

Not one to overlook a good thing, and without further delay Smith announced that he was taking over Skagway and would restore law and order to the community.

Soapy became the man in Skagway who championed rationality rather than violence. He had used diplomacy to save a man from the lynching mob so that the accused could be handed over to the proper officials of the government. Skagway businessmen were taking him to heart.

Some however, were most concerned, among them were the hard core of steely-eyed frontiersman, adventurers such as Frank Reid. Soapy's announcement caught them off guard including the early arrivals who had made a fortune selling and reselling Skagway's lots as surveyed by Reid, and who were apparently involved in other shady matters.

They decided something should be done immediately and formed the Committee of 101, which also included respected members of the community such as Major Strong, Si Tanner, Sam Lovell and others, but Frank Reid was the prime mover.

They immediately issued a public notice:

WARNING

A word to the wise should be sufficient. All confidence sharks, bunco men, sure-thing men, and all other objectionable characters are notified to leave Skagway and the White Pass. Failure to comply with this warning will be followed by prompt action.

Signed - COMMITTEE OF ONE HUNDRED AND ONE.

Smith was quick to realize that this could cause some of his many small business supporters to hesitate and possibly change their loyalty. He replied almost immediately with a bulletin of his own. Within a few hours of the posting of the Committee of 101 bulletins Smith had posted the town with his own placards inviting all interested to take part, not a closed session as was the Committee of l01 meeting, but open to all.

ANNOUNCEMENT
The business interests of Skagway propose to put a stop to the lawless acts of many newcomers. We hereby summon all good citizens to a meeting at which these matters will be discussed. Come one, come all. Immediate action will be taken for relief. Let this be a warning to those cheechakos who are disgracing our city. The Meeting will be held at Sylvester Hall at 8 p.m. sharp.

Signed: Jefferson R. Smith, Chairman.

Jeff Smith's reply, once again pointed him out as the one man who could restore law and order in Skagway. The turnout jammed the hall to overflowing. Smith opened the meeting with a fiery address using his God-given silk smooth voice and power of persuasion. He deplored the present conditions and pointed out that the scum and riff-raff from all over the world were coming to Skagway. He promised to form a real committee to show the crooks just who was running the town. He proposed a Committee of Three Hundred and Three, which was immediately passed by the throng, possibly spurred on by some of his close followers. He was then named permanent chairman of The Law and Order Committee and immediately posted signs throughout the town and up the trail.

PUBLIC WARNING

The body of men calling themselves the Committee of One Hundred and One are hereby notified that any overt act committed by them will be met promptly by the law abiding citizens of Skagway and each member and their property will be held responsible for any unlawful act on their part. The Law and Order Committee of Three Hundred and Three will see that justice is dealt out to its fullest extent and no Blackmailers or Vigilantes will be tolerated.

Signed: Law and Order Committee of Three Hundred and Three.

The forming of the two committees divided Skagway into two camps, those who championed the forces of Frank Reid and his followers and those who backed Jeff Smith.

There was no opposition to Smith's program, with the threat of confiscating of property proving to be a club over the Committee of 101 members who did not want a challenge of their property rights, especially those who had illegally garnered many of the lots following Reid's survey.

Soapy's brazen audacity and swift and resourceful reprisal resulted in making the original committee the butt of jokes and ridicule. Soon it was forgotten and once again Soapy had come out on top and ruled as "King of Skagway." Violent crime was practically eliminated, although lesser evils continued. Such remained the situation for approximately six months.

One of Smith's first orders on consolidating his power was never fleece or molest a permanent citizen. Only the transients. When some of his men sheared the youthful chief of the local fire department, Smith was aghast and returned the victim's money, and at the same time gave his followers a tongue-lashing. He also managed to exude an aura of law and order by halting minor crimes, misdemeanors and the like.

It was a well known fact that although Smith was the so-called "King of the Underworld" in Skagway, there were other gangs operating and not paying tribute to him. All were jealous of his success and position in the community.

A few ruffians who did not agree with Smith's orders temporarily moved out on the trails, but soon returned realizing that there was more profit and less risk in being part of one organization. Many accepted Smith as their protector and leader.

Soapy Smith was much in favor of the development of transportation over White Pass. On one occasion hoodlums blocked construction of the Brackett road. When George Brackettg went to government officials for help, he was told that there was nothing they could do. Brackett was on the verge of violence when Smith inquired of the problem. Without hesitation he went into action. He brought some of his "Indians", as he called them, to the scene and gave the hoodlums a limited number of hours to get out of the way or he would take action. There was no sight of the hoodlums the next morning and work continued without further problems.

During Smith's "reign" there were only two murders in Skagway compared to such as the Nevada rush following the days of '49 in California some years earlier. In Virginia City Mark Twain reported that the first 26 graves were occupied by murdered men. Established in 1868 Pioche, known as the wildest town in Nevada, saw 76 men die in fights over claims or imagined insults before anyone died of natural causes. During the years 1871/72 three out of five Nevadans who came to a violent death died in Pioche.

Nome too, during its glory days had its problems with many of the Skagway crowd going there but with no Soapy Smith to maintain order. As a result crime was uncontrolled. Will Ballou, a well-known Rampart businessman, reported there was a killing a day in Nome, with the comment."We had a dead man for breakfast almost every morning."

The first Skagway murder shortly after Soapy took over was when George Buchanon, manager of the Skagway Township Co. which "ran" the city and who was one of the original Committee of 101, fell in love with a lady restaurant owner. He was thwarted and spurned by his lady love so he shot her and then killed himself.

A hurriedly convened coroner's jury called it "murder from passion and suicide." The pair were promptly buried in the small Skagway cemetery.

The second was in May, when a black prostitute was strangled in her house, apparently for her money.

On January 31, one week after the Fay affair, the Committee of 101 petitioned Washington for federal troops and asked that the town be placed under martial law. Four companies of the 14th Calvary from Vancouver Barracks in Washington State were dispatched, arriving in Skagway from Portland on the SS Undine on February 25, 1898. Companies B and H under Col. Thomas MacAnderson were assigned to Dyea and A and G under Lt. Col. George B. Russell were assigned to Skagway. This tactic was short lived however, as one of the first things the federal troops did under martial law was shut down the saloons, dance halls and other entertainment centers. This brought about a halt to free spending by the sporting element, causing many legitimate businesses to suffer.

With the lifting of martial law, the primary duty for the soldiers became patrolling the White Pass and Chilkoot trails. They arrived, however, ill-equipped clothing-wise for such duty in mid-winter. Instead of coonskin caps, muskrat gloves and buffalo coats as used by troops in other northern posts, they were outfitted with campaign hats, regulation blue overcoats, white cotton gloves and light weight underwear. They had been in training for warmer climes in case there
was trouble with Spain. They almost froze to death, especially those a assigned to duty a mile or so up the Brackett Road or White Pass trail.

Members of the Committee of 101 acting as Vigilantes decided to take other steps to drive the underworld elements from town. A lengthy list of those to be expelled was drawn up, but Jeff Smith's name was not among those threatened. This because the business community tolerated him, and in some cases applauded him as he brought order out of chaos. The Vigilantes apparently all but disbanded for the time being.

CHAPTER 17
LIKES ATTRACT

About the time that Soapy took over Skagway he became associated with another newcomer. He was the black sheep of a rich and prominent San Francisco area family - a family that had founded three towns in California. His father had been a '49er prospector, lawyer and U.S. Minister to Guatemala.

He was Wilson Mizner, who had spent considerable time on San Francisco's Barbary Coast and who came north to assist his brother Edgar, an official of the Alaska Commercial Company sent to Skagway to take care of company matters there and throughout the Territory.

Wilson, however, disliked work. His philosophy, like that of Jeff, was that one should turn to every conceivable plan for skinning a fellow player without actually robbing him. The penalties for robbery were far too severe to make it sensible, but the means of chiseling just within the law were endless and always at one's barked elbow.

Having a keen sense in acquiring money, it was said that Mizner could hear from the tenth floor of a building the "plunk" of a $10 bill dropped onto a plush carpet.

A history of the Mizner family notes that "Wilson had already received training from the masters of the underworld. In Skagway he received a polishing and finishing from the greatest American professor of sharp practices, gentle larceny, and all-around crime, the celebrated Jefferson Randolph (Soapy) Smith, the real life American version of the Man Who Would Be King.

Soapy and Wilson were attracted to each other by the natural law that causes celebrities to gravitate in one another's society. Mizner traveled through life in a caravan of headliners. Besides such as Soapy, Diamond Tooth Gertie, and the Half-Way Kid, there was an assort-

Wilson Mizner, quite a con-man before meeting Soapy, gives full credit to Smith for his becoming one of the greatest American professors of sharp practices, gentle larceny and all-around crime. Of all of Mizner's idols and mentors, none had a greater influence on him than Soapy. - Clifford Collection.

A lover of turmoil and arrogance, Joe Boyle was probably the only person to insult Soapy Smith in his own Parlors and get away with it. In later years Boyer secured most of the valuable claims in Dawson and become King of the Klondike. - Clifford Collection

ment of Vanderbilts, duPonts, Stotesburys and Wideners. Also O. Henry, George M. Cohan, Irving Berlin, and Buffalo Bill, as well as the kings of reporters and press agents. There was also John McGaw, W.C. Fields, Damon Runyan, Bat Masterson and most of the stars of stage, screen and Tin Pan Alley. He was also the friend of gamblers, bunco steerers, fences and international crooks.

Of all of Mizner's idols and mentors, none had a greater influence on him than Soapy. Wilson spent two months with Jeff in Skagway before moving on to Dawson City and Nome.

Mizner delighted in telling the story of a time Soapy was arrested in Chicago on a charge of operating with confederates and obtaining money under false pretenses. According to Wilson, the judge was confused, claiming he couldn't make heads or tails out of the testimony and requested that Soapy show him how he worked and let the police officers tell how the law was violated.

Soapy wrapped several pieces of soap, first putting a $50 bill around one of them, requested that the judge pay him 25 cents and pick one of the bars of soap.

The judge handed over a quarter and took the $50 cake, folded the bill and placed it in his vest pocket.

Then he read the riot act to the police about hounding an honest businessman pursuing his lawful calling, explaining that his merchandising methods were obviously fair and honorable. He dismissed the case. This was the era in history when surprise gifts and the like were all the rage in packaging.

Mizner went on to Dawson where he became saloon partner with Swiftwater Bill Gates and later Tex Rickard in Dawson, and followed him to Nome and Goldfield. Rickard later built the famous Madison Square Garden in New York.

CHAPTER 18
THE LADY AND THE GAMBLER

It was late-April 1898 that a Salvation Army delegation, headed by 32-year old Evangeline Booth, daughter of its founder General Wallace Booth, arrived in Skagway from Vancouver, B.C. on the S.S. Tee. They disembarked to be greeted by a large crowd and marched down the gang plank and led a parade uptown to the corner of Broadway and Holly Sts. between the Pack Train Saloon and Jeff Smith's Parlors.

There was a street meeting on the spot. It was a chilly evening and as is often the case at that time of year, a cold wind blew down from the Chilkat range, causing Evangeline Booth to shiver as she preached.

Quietly a man made his way to where she was standing, draped a blanket over her shoulders and whispered, "Soapy said to put it around you."

In her mind this could not be from the Soapy Smith that she had heard so much about, the evil man who had cast his spell over Denver, Creede and other Western mining towns before heading for Skagway to continue his evil ways. A conman who headed an army of thugs, tin horn gamblers, sharpers, bunco artists, shell game operators and disreputable women. A man whose victims where the newly-arrived stampeders on the way to or from the Klondike.

Nor could this be the man who had taken over the town, bringing about the forming of a Vigilante committee which posted a notice ordering all "objectionable characters out of the area."

As she continued preaching, Miss Eva noticed a man, with a pushed-back black sombrero riding a big white stallion to the edge of the crowd. He listened with inter-

Evangeline Booth, daughter of the founder of the Salvation Army, made a futile attempt to "save" Soapy Smith when her group stopped off in Skagway enroute to Dawson City. - Salvation Army.

Mattie Silks, queen of the Denver madams, made a small fortune in Dawson, but thanks in part to Soapy Smith struck out and departed in haste when she tried to set up shop in Skagway.
- Clifford Collection.

est. This man was Soapy Smith.

Evangeline continued her nightly meetings, attracting crowds which she described as sinners. They cheered and clapped as she stepped up to speak, and she talked for an hour or more at each meeting, pleading with them to forsake their sins and accept salvation through Christ. They raised their hands and asked her to pray for them.

Each night Jeff Smith was also present and made large donations to the Salvation Army. One night he tossed a gold coin onto the drum to start the collection. On another he sent a large slab of moose meat for the Army to use to feed the starving and hungry in Skagway. "God had nothing to do with the meat," a note stated. "Compliments of Jeff's Place."

This was a different Jeff Smith. It was the Smith who raised funds to build churches, provide monies for widows and children, asked each Skagway citizen to adopt one of the thousands of dogs" that had been brought in by prospectors and abandoned in town when it was found that they could not pack loads over the White Pass Trail. It was the Smith who had never killed a person in his life, but who had shown his temper in doing physical harm when the editor of a Denver newspaper printed insulting remarks about his wife. This was the Jeff Smith who in his younger days seriously considered taking to the ministry.

The Salvation Army had pitched its tents among some trees on the outskirts of town. One evening the Mounties, who had accompanied the group and who had been assigned to guard Miss Eva, were told that Soapy Smith and five of his followers were coming.

"Leave him to me," Evangeline said as she walked out to invite the men to have a cup of cocoa. As they stood around the campfire, she took Soapy aside.

"Why don't you give up this kind of life?" she inquired.

"I can't," he said. "if they didn't think I would kill them,there's plenty who would kill me."

"There are worse things than death," Ms. Booth replied. "Stop taking lives, God wants to give you life."

"You talk like my mother," Smith replied. "She took me to Salvation Army meetings when I was a boy. I liked it. They let me clap my hands when we sang. It seemed so long ago — so long ago."

Quietly in the flickering shadows of the campfire, Evangeline Booth talked to Jefferson Randolph Smith about Jesus Christ. For three hours they sat, until finally Soapy bowed his head as the English woman prayed. They returned to the group and Soapy motioned his men to their horses and they hastily mounted and rode away.

The Salvation Army evangelist had set out to do what no one else thought possible — convert the "wickedest" man in Alaska.

The question was, did Evangeline Booth succeed? Had their discussion opened the Life-gate for Soapy Smith? Had her testimony penetrated the weak spot in his armor? He had listened and he had hesitated — but was it too late?

It was possible that Soapy Smith had been touched by the meeting and no longer had the fear of death. Perhaps so. Historians will never know. Things happen too fast.

CHAPTER 19
ALASKA MILITIA

In the spring of 1898 the Spanish conflict aroused the patriotism in "Colonel" Smith to the point that he decided to recruit a company of soldiers in Skagway such as Teddy Roosevelt's Rough Riders.

Such became legal under authorization of the Volunteer Bill of April 23, 1898. The bill as presented by President William McKinley provided for the First Volunteer Cavalry Regiment — The Rough Riders — as a result of the sinking of the battleship Maine in Havana harbor on Feb. 15, 1898 with the loss of 260 of her crew.

President McKinley called for 125,000 volunteers from the seven Western states and territories, a figure that was soon raised to 267,000. Three regiments were to be raised in the West, the first in the four territories which included Alaska, the second in Wyoming and the third in the Dakotas.

Playing an important part in Smith's decision must have been the fact that Sen. Frances E. Warren of Wyoming had introduced a bill in Congress authorizing funds for such units. Upon formation of the Wyoming unit on March 8, 1898 Secretary of War Russell A. Alger allocated $250,000 for organizational expenses, $197,000 for transportation and horses, $31,392 for equipment and $15,000 for subsistence. The Wyoming unit was formed but it never saw action.

Alaska recruits were not limited to Soapy's followers. Skagway was full of newly arrived but stranded gold seekers who saw such as an opportunity to get back to the States and eventually home at government expense. Soapy had no trouble signing them up.

As soon as the unit, known as Company A, 1st Regiment of National Guard of Alaska was complete, Smith was elected Captain, John Foley one of the town's better three-card-monte dealers 1st Lieutenant, J.T. Miller the bouncer at Clancy's 1st sergeant, and the head bartender at the Klondike Saloon chaplain. Smith cornered all the silk ribbon in town and made badges for those involved. Running short of such material late arrivals received badges made of butcher paper, but all were treated equally proclaiming them members of the Alaska Guards.

So sincere was Smith in his patriotic fervor that he was both mortified and infuriate when, in his commendable design to come to the rescue of the United States, he was double-crossed. This was accomplished by a gang of false patriots who went about enrolling men for the military service and taking them into a back room of a saloon for physical examinations. While a scoundrel fake "medico" put the

Skaguay, Alaska, March 19,1898.

To Hon. William McKinley,

President of the United States,

Washington, D.C.,

Sir:-- I take pleasure in enclosing for your perusal the minutes and enrollment of the Skaguay Military Company, organized for the purpose of responding to any call you may make for volunteers in the event of war with Spain.

It is the desire of the Company to commence drilling at once, having secured the services of an ex-army officer for that purpose and we wish to know if we may be furnished with the necessary arms, accouterments, etc., for that purpose. This organization, we hope, will become a permanent one and one which will not be far behind any other organization of this kind in responding to the demand in time of trouble. I am,

Very respectfully,

Your obedient servant,

[signature: Jeff R Smith]

When war with Spain became a possibility, Jeff Smith organized the Alaska Guards. This letter offered President William McKinley the services of the guards should there be a need for them.
- Clifford Collection.

April 9, 1898.

Dear Sir:

The President directs me to acknowledge the receipt of your communication of the 19th ultimo, enclosing the minutes and enrollment of the Skaguay Military Company, organised for the purpose of responding to a call for volunteers in the event that they should be needed, and to inform you that it has been referred for the consideration of the Secretary of War.

Very truly yours,

Secretary to the President. ✱

Capt. Jeff R. Smith,
  Skaguay, Alaska.

The White House responded to Smith's letter thanking him for the offer of the services of the Alaska Guards. The letter is signed by John Addison Porter, Secretary to the President. Soapy proudly displayed the letter in Jeff's Parlors.
- Clifford Collection.

stripped candidates through stunts to test their health, deft fingers of his accomplices searched the pockets of the volunteer's discarded garb and removed all cash and valuables.

This dastardly work was reported to Soapy, who wrathfully ordered the perpetrators rounded up and hailed before him. Caught red-handed, they attempted to laugh it off, that their performance was a practical joke and they stated that they intended to return the loot. The excuse was not accepted. Soapy compelled them to disgorge their ill-gotten booty on the spot and return it to the rightful owners, after which the culprits were forced to apologize to their victims and accept an unpleasant tongue-lashing from Smith. It included a warning that any repetition of the deed would result in their immediate banishment from Skagway.

After many days of drilling, Capt. Smith decided that the Alaska Guards should parade through town the evening of Sunday, May 1, 1898, Skagway's first such parade. It started on the waterfront with Capt. Smith, mounted on a white horse heading up the unit. A band, recruited from the various saloons was placed in the middle of the marching men so that all could hear the music.

Things went without a hitch until they reached 5th and Broadway where Capt. Smith and the lead unit turned right and the band and rear unit left. They got back together at 7th and State. Another interruption occurred in front of the Princess Hotel when Babe Davenport and her girls demanded that a Women's Auxiliary be formed but the suggestion was ignored. The parade lasted an hour and one-half, breaking up in front of City Hall where several patriotic citizens addressed the group, General Weyler was hung in effigy and Capt. Smith, closed the session with an inspirational address, " You are fine brave

FREEDOM

FOR

CUBA.

REMEMBER

The Maine!

Compliments of . . .

THE SKAGUAY

MILITARY CO

JEFF R. SMITH, CAPT.

Ribbon provided by Capt. Jeff Smith for members of the Alaska Guards who took part in Skagway's first parade the evening of May 1, 1898. - J.J. Smith Collection.

78

men, each and every one of you, and I am sure that you will unhesitatingly follow me anywhere and at any time." With that he headed for Jeff's Place and was followed by a majority of the "troops" who were in need of quenching their thirst. Needless to say the saloon did a land-office business for the next few hours.

The parade had been proceeded by a letter to President William McKinley to the effect that Skagway's Alaska Guards were ready to move against Spain as soon as funds for their transportation were received. Soapy received a reply from the White House and was informed that his offer had been forwarded to Secretary of War Russell A. Alger who replied immediately, thanking Smith but pointing out that it would be both impossible and impractical to put the Guards into service immediately. Smith proudly posted the Secretary's reply in Jeff's Parlors for all to see. The unit appeared in the July 4th parade and continued to drill until the war danger was over.

A short time after the parade Smith organized a benefit show to create a fund for the future widows and orphans of the Guard members. Some 1450 tickets were sold at $1 each. The benefit was a gala success but unfortunately the "treasurer" disappeared with the female "star" of the show before the funds could be accounted for.

Soapy Smith celebrated along with others in Jeffs Parlors following the Alaska Guards parade the evening of May 1, 1898. It was one of the few times that he so indulged. The only other person identified other than Soapy in the foreground is Nate Pollock the bartender. - Clifford Collection.

CHAPTER 20
MORE THAN ONE SOAPY

On May 2, 1898 the Seattle Post Intelligence carried a story of an incident in nearby Tacoma. A group of soldiers from Camp John Rogers made a raid on a group of sure-thing gamblers who opened their games just north of the encampment.

The following day the Tacoma Ledger carried the story, noting that "the gang was generally reputed to be Soapy Smith's crowd from Skagway and that Soapy was reported to be among them, although this could not be verified."

Wire services carried the story headlining the "fact" that Soapy Smith was among a group of eight sure-thing gamblers arrested by the military outside of Tacoma.

The arrests were made at 2 p.m. on May 1, 1898 and the group spent the night in the County jail before being sent on their way. Soapy could not have been among them as on the evening of May 1 Smith was leading his Skagway Guards on their "famous" parade through the streets of the gold rush community. This is one of many examples where Jeff Smith was blamed for crimes and actions that he had nothing to do with.

This particular incident was explained when some of Smith's

Skagway during the days of the Gold Rush when population reached 15,000 or more. - Clifford Collection.

correspondence was located after his demise and was published in the Alaska-Yukon Magazine, Dec. 1907/Jan. 1908.

Harry Green, one of Smith's early day associates had passed himself off as Soapy on a trip to the Pacific Northwest. When Soapy learned of it he wrote a scalding letter to the culprit. The reply, dated April 12, 1898 apologized for such action and Green explained that in Smith's making it pretty warm for him he stated that he never intended to return to Skagway.

The letter is as follows:

HOTEL NORTHERN
Seattle, Wash.

April 12, 1898
Mr. Smith:
Your letter of the 28th just received by chance I
happened to drop into Seattle today.

When I left Skaguay on 21st Mar. I left on the boat Ning Chaw and there was no one on that boat but a lot of your friends, some fellows as Luther Woods, Johnnie Miller, Bill Toregdy and Big Down, a lot of Arizona and Texas friends of yours and mine, this talk that was made to the reporter was made all through a josh, they named on the boat to the reporter Luther Woods name was supposed to be Jerry Daily, my name supposed to be Jeff Smith, brother Big Down supposed to be Harry Green. Roberts partner they asked for Harry Green on the boat running from Victoria to Seattle, they referred the reporter to Big Down that was supposed to be Harry Green, the man that come back from fish creek, with a lot of big nugget, a wealthy man, now you can see the crowd on the boat that was doing a lot for a josh on the reporter than anything else. You have never known me to be a knocker of no body living. I don't like a reporter or policeman any how. The reporter in Victoria had it that Soapy Smiths gang got run out of Skaguay and we were supposed to be the gang, for myself I did not care, because I like all kinds of money myself, so for that reason I don't want you to think I implicated in giving the reporter such a interview. In regards to making it pretty warm for me when I return. I never intended to go back when I left down there and if I ever happen to get back, I'll not hide from no body. I have not done it yet and never will, there is as good a blood in me as there is in any body there that you will find me at Seattle or Spokane at any time. I am sorry that I have to write this kind of a letter because
I have a lot of friends amongst you fellows, such as Agerman Daily and all others that I know. I don't want them to think for one moment

that I was to fault for any josh like that, no more news.

Remain yours

HARRY GREEN.

The Seattle Post Intelligencer, which published more news on the Klondike rush than any other publication, reported "Three fourths of the stories written about "Soapy" Smith have been fiction. He often said that he learned things in the newspapers about himself and of his doing that he had no knowledge.

The story continued, "He had a heart larger than all out doors, and he would stand by a friend through thick and thin. He has been falsely credited with killing eight men, although he had never killed a man and had been lucky in escaping several attempts to murder him. Several times news reports were published of Smith's death."

The NWMP official report stated that it was impossible that Smith and his gang were guilty of every crime committed between Lynn Canal and the Canadian border, although for each offense for which there was no known agent blame was ascribed to him. The report went on to point out that on the score of justice, this makes little difference, for Smith was in truth a master of treachery, an expert at exploiting the line between the law and its omissions, and a practitioner of nearly every form of devilment. He raised to a fine art the perpetration of crime, and if he passed up a "good thing," it was by accident rather that design. In many respects he deserved a place in The Chamber of Horrors of Madam Tussaud's wax exhibition.

Others of the press, such as William Saportas of the New York World who eventually went to work for Smith, described him in print as, "the most gracious, kind hearted man I've ever met." and added "to know him is to like him."

Edward F. Cahill of the San Francisco Examiner, reported "Soapy Smith is not a dangerous man." and told the outside world, "He is not a desperado. He is not a scoundrel. He is not a criminal." Cahill reported that Smith was cool, fearless, generous and honorable and wrote "He bitterly resents the imputations that he is a thief and a vagrant."

Sylvester Scovel of the New York World wrote, "Smith may be a grafter, but he is one of the most generous, kind-hearted men I have ever met in my life. He is always ready to help those in distress and he loves his family. To know Smith is to like him."

In an interview after Smith's death, Harry Sage of San Diego, who was well acquainted with Soapy in Skagway, stated,

"He never turned down a hungry man. He was a sharper, but he was as gullible as any of the suckers, particularly so when someone told him a hard-luck story. He had an idea that it was up to him to help everybody and found he had a mighty big job on his hands. He even staked the dance hall girls when they were broke, and he contributed heavily to the churches he helped to start. Any down-and-outer who couldn't raise a nickel anywhere else went to Soapy and never failed to make a touch."

Smith kept in touch with the outside world, and especially the underworld, through a remarkable correspondence which ranged from the Pacific Northwest to Central America. He received letters from politicians, lawyers, police officials, professional men, journalists, magazine editors and crooks. The great and the near great.

There were a couple of letters from Cy Warman who was publisher of the Creede Candle while Soapy was there and who became editor of McClure's Magazine. He requested that Soapy set up an interview for him with California's gentleman highway bandit Black Bart (Charles E. Bolton) following Bart's release from prison in 1888. He apparently settled in St. Louis where he became a friend of Soapy's.

Jeff's correspondence formed an endless chain, a sort of continental spy-network, and he carefully pasted every letter into a huge scrapbooks which he kept up to date and concealed in a drawer in his old fashioned roll top desk.

The scrapbook was turned over to Marshal Tanner who apparently sold the letters to Alaska-Yukon Magazine which started publishing them in the December 1907 and January 1908 issues. They were entitled "Correspondence of a Crook" and were under the byline of Robert D. Jones. Although the magazine indicated that the series would continue in following issues, the letters apparently disappeared. A substantial reward for the return of letters later was offered by the Smith family but they were never located.

CHAPTER 21
GALA SENDOFF

Shortly after the Alaska Guard's parade the regular U.S. troops assigned to the Skagway area were ordered back to their barracks at Vancouver, Wash. to prepare for transfer to Manila. As they marched through Skagway to board the steamer Queen, few if any, residents paid attention to their departure.

Not so with patriotic Soapy Smith. When he noted the lack of interest he visited the various saloons, theaters and dance halls giving a rousing speech on patriotism and "ordered" those in attendance, including the various bands and musical organizations, to go down to the dock and give the soldiers a royal sendoff. Not to be forgotten was an ample supply of "refreshments."

When the soldiers heard the bands marching down to the dock they came out on deck, and were joined aboard the ship by the many merrymakers down to see them off. For more than two hours it was a gala celebration under Soapy Smith's direction, so much so that a half dozen Skagway citizens were still aboard when the Queen departed and later were put ashore in Juneau.

Soapy was a proud man and for the most part was treated with respect when he offered to be friendly with newcomers. One such meeting saw him receiving a different reception. With Joe Boyle, well known in the sporting world, and who later became known as the King of the Klondike, such was not the case.

While visiting Soapy's Place Jeff invited him to have a drink. Boyle responded, "No thanks. I don't drink with strangers and I only know you by your reputation." His inflection was a gross insult as he rocked back and forth on his heels.

Boyle was camped out in a tent on the beach and that evening he was attacked by four ruffians, said to have been members of Smith's gang. Things did not go well with the locals as two of them were beat to a pulp and the other two escaped. Joe and some of the others on the beach, dragged the pair back to Smith's Place and tossed them onto the bar, remarking to Soapy, "After this keep your murderous rats out of my road and you keep your hands off of me." Boyle was not bothered again.

Boyle's partner was Frank Slavin, a heavyweight fighter of world championship ability and with whom Boyle frequently sparred. He was with Boyle in Skagway, but whether he was on the beach that evening was not reported. Another partner who was present was Jack Holt, who later became a movie star.

Boyle made a fortune in the Klondike, formed and led a company of Canadian volunteers to fight in World War I, was a British spy in Russia during the revolution and rescued the Rumanian crown jewels from the Soviets. He became a close friend and confidant of Queen Marie of Rumania.

Through the winter months and early into spring while the White Pass was closed, Dyea and the Chilkoot Pass, with its more direct but steeper route and aerial tram lines, proved to be a strong competitor for Skagway and the White Pass Trail and later the Brackett Haul Road. All this came to an end, however, when on April 3, 1898 a snow slide on the Chilkoot Pass resulted in more than 60 deaths. From then on the White Pass and Skagway with the haul road started in November 1897 and followed by the construction of the White Pass & Yukon Route railroad in 1898 became the favored route to the Klondike. Dyea gradually sank into the sunset. Nothing but a few pilings and scrap remain today.

When Denver's famous madam, Mattie Silks, with a dozen of her most beautiful girls headed for the Klondike in the spring of 1898 she avoided Skagway in favor of Dyea because her husband Cort Thompson and Soapy were bitter enemies because of previous clashes. This despite the fact that she and Soapy had been good friends in Denver.

Fearing the winter — especially because of her husband's health — Mattie left Dawson after less than a 90 day stay. Asked how she had done, she stated that it was more than she had ever done before ($38,000 profit) even after paying all expenses, passage both ways for the entire group, protection money and Cort's enormous gambling debts.

Later Mattie reported, "The protection money I paid in Denver was penny-ante stuff along side what the Redcoats (North West Mounted Police) demanded," according to a Denver friend.

"I had to pay $50 a day for every day I operated in Dawson, but I'm not kicking. It was worth it."

After paying Mattie 50 percent for board, each of the girls was earning $30 to $50 a day. Mattie's expenses were high, but her total receipts were enormous. Her sales of liquid refreshments brought huge profits. Champagne was $30 a bottle and her "boarders" received $5 for each bottle. Whiskey was 50 cents a shot, mostly moonshine made from alcohol. Miners paid a dollar for a drink and a dance. The music never stopped, day or night.

Mattie also took along her old gold scales she had in Colorado with the little square of carpet that caught the dust "spilled" from the scales.

Cort chuckled about the way they got the miners drunk, and rolled them for their dust. He reported two Swedes, who had been parted from some $50,000 worth of dust, made so much trouble with the authorities that it was necessary for them to get rid of the loot. They buried it somewhere out in the timber country, but the officers kept such a close watch on them that they were scared to take it when they left for the States. It's still buried up there somewhere.

On the way back, Mattie decided to stop in Skagway to look into the possibilities of opening up shop, if they could come to peaceful terms with Soapy. This despite the fact that six-foot tall Lil Davenport of Chicago was the madam of Skagway's principal parlorhouse and queen of the red light district. She accumulated a fortune in Klondike gold and discouraged any competition in Skagway.

The plan did not work out, as Mattie reported upon arriving in Seattle a few days later. She stated that upon arrival in Skagway she learned that Ella Nita Wilson, a mulatto prostitute, had been murdered in her house and a large trunk, supposed to have contained her money was broken into. Despite reports to the contrary, this was only the second murder to be committed in "crime ridden" Skagway after Soapy Smith took over.

Deputy United States Marshal S.S. Taylor took charge of the body and was investigating the murder. Mattie reported that she occupied a room in the Occidental Hotel adjoining one that served as an office for the Marshal. Only a partition of thin boards separated the two rooms and she stated that the night after the murder she heard Marshal Taylor, "Soapy" Smith, Bill Tanner and one Bowers, the latter two well known crooks, talking in Taylor's office while dividing up money. She gathered from the conversation that the money was from Ella Wilson and that the murder had been committed by Tanner and Bowers at the instigation and consent of Taylor and Smith.

But that was not all. Mrs. Silks says that while she sat in her room she heard the outfit planned to strangle her to death in the same way that Ella Wilson had been served. After hearing this plot Mattie came to the conclusion that Skagway had become too hot to hold her and she took her departure on the Farallon, the first ship available.

Marshal Taylor and Smith filed libel suits of $25,000 damages against Mattie and the Seattle Times which published the story. Upon Smith's death and Taylor's arrest, the paper stated that it felt vindicated for its actions.

CHAPTER 22
SOAPY GOES PROSPECTING

The occasion arose where Smith and his cohorts were involved in attempting to "mine" gold from the Yukon as it was being transported to Victoria in Canada or other West Coast ports. It also involved the North West Mounted Police.

The Mounties had stationed police, "foreigners without jurisdiction," in Skagway from Oct. 20, 1896 in an effort to protect their claim as to whereabouts of the border between Alaska and the Yukon. That office was closed on May 11, 1897 and the men, under Inspector Zachary Taylor Wood, grandson of U.S. President Zachary Taylor, moved to Lake Bennett, 25 miles inside Canadian territory.

At the same time orders were received to transfer $27,488 in customs collections to Victoria. Superintendent Col. S.B. Steele and Wood were much concerned over getting the funds down the trail and aboard ship in Skagway safely in view of Smith's control of the area and his men ever watching the trails and stationed aboard inbound and outbound ships.

It was decided that using an armed escort down the trail, which could account for considerable problems and possibly death or wounding of many should a holdup be attempted was out. Instead, Wood volunteered to undertake the assignment - under the pretext that he was being transferred back to the free life of patrol work on the open prairies. Such would explain why an officer in good health was being transferred from the area when the workload was increasing.

Quietly, expertly, for the express benefit of Soapy Smith, rumors began to fly that "Zac" Wood was pulling stakes permanently for Calgary and was to be accompanied to Skagway with enough boatmen to carry his luggage to the steamer.

In the meantime $130,000 in gold and other funds as well pay vouchers were added, bringing the total shipment to approximately a quarter of a million dollars. Inspector Wood, along with Constables William Chalmers and Frederick Young wearing fatigues, headed across Lake Linderman and down the trail on June 9 toting two Gladstones and police dunnage bags. They used the less traveled Chilkoot Trail rather than the overcrowded White Pass and hired Sam Heron's pack train to carry the luggage. They passed quickly through Sheep Camp, a relay station of several thousand people and reputed to be the most lawless part of the trail and where gamblers made a final try at the cheechakos heading for the Yukon.

They arrived at Dyea at 7 o'clock in the evening and overnight in a tar paper shack in an area were idle soldiers were billeted.

Learning that the SS Tartar would not arrive in Skagway for three days they moved to the the less vulnerable Olympic Hotel where Wood and his partners stood guard over the treasure 24 hours a day. Sgt. James Green, another NWMP officer along with Dr. H.B.Runnalls (who served as postmaster in Skagway) rowed over from Skagway and reported that Soapy and his men apparently were aware that something was up.

Following a conference with C.P.R. officials it was decided to charter a private boat to move the gold rather than using the regular ferry service between Dyea and Skagway. Early in the morning of the fourth day they set sail aboard a local tug, the Lady of the Lake.

Soapy apparently was well aware of the moves and in mid-bay a small boat of rough necks bore down astern of the tug as it chugged on it way to Skagway. As the boat neared the tug, Sgt. George A. Pringle and Constable Chalmers shouldered their carbines and shouted a warning for the boat to keep its distance. The ruffians dropped back out of bullet range.

The Lady of the Lake anchored in the Skagway harbor and Capt. Pybus on the Tartar had his crew on the bridge, armed with rifles as the gold was taken by rowboat to the wharf for transfer to the Tartar. On the wharf Inspector Wood and his men were greeted by Soapy Smith along with "Slim Jim " Foster, the "Sheeney Kid," "Red," Old Man Tripp and Turner Jackson. It was obvious that Smith had been tipped off on the gold shipment. It was a touchy moment.

A gruff command split the air. There was the echo of marching feet. A squad of Royal Naval Reservists at the double and fully armed — an armed force on foreign soil that was never questioned by those versed in international law — came to the rescue.

The rest was an anti-climax. With a smile Jeff Smith invited the Inspector to visit the town, but Wood graciously declined. After the gold was safely stowed in the ship's bullion room, Inspector Wood did go ashore until the ship sailed at 1 p.m. with Constable Chalmers also aboard. The fortune was delivered to the Bank of British Columbia in Victoria five days later.

Soapy's web extended beyond Skagway with informants on most of the ships plying between Alaska and the West Coast. Some of his agents prowled the trails to the gold fields working minor cons on the cheechakos and getting a line on what the boys were bringing back. The agents, disguised as prospectors and sported genuine beards, filled their packs with straw instead of heavy camping equipment, which they didn't need as they returned to the comforts of Skagway each evening.

As work on the railroad over White Pass increased one of the strict orders set as a safety measure by Michael J. Heney, construction chief for the White Pass & Yukon Route railroad, was that there be no liquor and no smoking as well as no gambling allowed in the camps.

Such had not escaped Soapy Smith's attention and one of the first things he did was send a member of his group to set up a tent with a plentiful supply of liquor and gambling equipment along the route but outside the camp areas.

When Heney learned of the tent's existence, he ordered the gambler off the premises only to have the latter contend that he had as much right as anyone to be there.

In no mood to haggle, Heney contacted Hugh Foy, construction foreman, and pointing to a huge rock above the tent site, told him in a loud voice, "I want that rock out of there by five in the morning," and walked away.

Early the next morning Foy found the tent still occupied by Smith's aide sleeping soundly inside. He ordered his powderman to set a few sticks of dynamite under the rock and then wake up the tent's occupant and inform him that the rock would be blown up in five minutes. The tent occupant refused to move. Foy then took charge, stating, "In one minute by my watch I will give the order to touch off the fuse. It will burn for sixty seconds and then there will be an explosion and the rock will be here before you can blink an eye."

The gambler's only comment was "Go to Hell."

Foy gave the command, "Fire" and immediately ducked to safety behind a large rock. Ten seconds later he was joined by the tent's occupant. Together they watched the blast destroy the rock, tent, games and liquor.

Foy went to Heney and informed him that the rock was down.

"Good. What happened to the man?" was his comment.

"The last I saw him he was cussing a blue streak as he headed down the trail in his underwear.

That was the last time that there was any serious challenge of Heney's no liquor, no gambling order along the trail.

One of Soapy's ploys was to have returning gold laden prospectors deliver a letter to someone in Jeff's Parlors. This was a tipoff that they carried a considerable poke of gold. The rest was easy for the "skilled craftsmen" in Skagway.

Such was reported by Edward B. Lung, an unemployed Tacoma accountant, who had headed north prior to the arrival of the gold-ship Portland. On his return from the Klondike over the White Pass with a sizable amount of gold in his poke he told of being approached by a rough-looking character at the White Pass Hotel at Porcupine Hill. Upon

A group of Soapy Smith's followers and their dog, one of many adopted in Smith's successful "Adopt A Dog" campaign. Literally thousands of dogs were brought north to serve as sled dogs but were turned loose on Skagway streets to fend for themselves.- Clifford Collection.

learning he had come from the Klondike and was headed for Skagway, Lung was asked if he would deliver a letter in Skagway.

As a courtesy to another on the trail, Lung agreed. Upon arriving in Skagway he noted that the letter was addressed to a Mr. Y.M. Hopkins at Jeff's Parlors, 317 Holly St.

Lung delivered the letter and as a token of his appreciation Hopkins, one of the rougher members of Soapy's followers who had been a bodyguard for a wealthy Chinese in the vicious San Francisco tong wars, appeared delighted with the news in the letter. He insisted that Lung join his friends at the bar for a round of drinks in token of the appreciation.

Lung objected, stating he had to catch a boat to Seattle. He was immediately surrounded by Hopkins' friends, who refused to let him leave. Realizing that a trap was closing in on him, Lung made a desperate dash for the door and succeeded in escaping and ran for the waterfront.

It was later that he learned that other prospectors, returning with gold, had similar experiences, but were not so lucky in escaping and that by the time they left Jeff's Parlors, they had either lost their gold in a game of some sort or another, were involved in a fight during which their poke was taken, or even drugged and finding themselves out back without their gold when they awoke.

Such was noted by another rich returning Klondiker, Jim Georghegan who went through Skagway without any trouble, seeing neither Soapy or any of his henchmen. His comment was, "If you don't drink, you don't get robbed or rolled."

Some of the so-called rough stuff in Jeff's Place apparently was put on for the cheechakos.

Prospector John Ver Mehr, who lectured about the Trail of '98 for many years after the gold rush, liked to tell of his experiences in Soapy's Place. He and his two partners, enroute to the gold fields via Dyea during the hectic days of the rush, stopped off in Skagway to give the town the once-over.

They made a bee-line to Soapy Smith's saloon, knowing it was the first thing friends would ask about when they returned home.

They did not see Soapy, but were in his headquarters. They reported that it was a big disappointment as it looked like an ordinary saloon and they didn't see anyone who even looked crooked in the place.

"We called for our drinks and paid, then as we were about to throw the liquor down, a volley of shots let loose that raised us off our heels. Wasn't anything. Just some of the men shooting off their revolvers to scare us greenhorns. They called us 'cheechakos' and they all had a big laugh on us. They saw that they had scared us bug-eyed. We beat it and went back to our ship. Never in our lives had we been shot at before.

Others who visited Soapy's during the rush were victims of the same pranks, but were less inclined to admit that they had been the butt of a local joke. Their stories back home were of the 'ruffians' who did someone in at Jeff Smith's Parlor.

CHAPTER 23
HELPING HAND

Martin Itjen, early day Skagway business man, tells of an incident where a packer on the trail was hired to find a sick man and bring him back to Skagway. The packer picked four men to help and had to pay them ten dollars each, only to find that the man who had hired him had lost all his money gambling.

As was often the case with such happenings, the packer went to Soapy who replaced the $40 and then dug down into his own pocket to provide funds for the sick man and his companion to purchase tickets back to the lower states.

This, according to Itjen, "was the sort of man Soapy really was."

Itjen later became famous when, as a "true Alaskan" he accepted an invitation from Mae West to come down and visit her in Hollywood. In later years he started the "Skagway Streetcar" tours and acquired Soapy's Place and opened it as a museum.

On another occasion in the early summer of 1898 the daughter of Frank Webster, Skagway businessman and one of the leaders of the Committee of 101, wandered away from home in the maze of tents and woods on the outskirts of Skagway.

Her frantic mother was unable to find her and the father was in a session with the Vigilante's discussing the "future" of Soapy Smith in Skagway," a fact that Soapy was well aware of at the time.

Mrs. Webster was in despair when she heard a horse cantering up to her house. A bearded man dressed all in black mounted on a dapple gray horse had the little girl in front of him on the saddle. Soapy had learned that the youngster was missing and immediately started searching for her on his own.

He handed the little girl down to her mother and commented that Skagway wasn't a good place to let a little girl run loose. Soapy Smith had returned her safe and sound to her worried mother.

The situation at Skagway in the spring and summer of 1898 was described by S.H. Graves, president of the White Pass & Yukon Route in a report to the British backers in London:

"Winter has blocked the White Pass and closed the Yukon River, so the rush of gold seekers had accumulated on the coast where they were unloaded by the steamers. The country between the sea and Log Cabin, 30 miles inland including the White Pass, was hotly claimed by both Canada and the United States, but the latter held de facto possession with a company of soldiers at Dyea. Canada kept two or three mounted police in Skagway to support a claim to possession, but they were not allowed to exercise jurisdiction and had merely the status of private individuals. The town-site was claimed by a Company, but was in the possession of more than ten thousand squatters in tents and wooden shanties. There was no law under which any municipal government could be organized, nor was there any Federal law, or courts, or police, or authority. The only representative of the Federal Government was an official known under the imposing title of "Deputy United States Marshal." He was in fact in league with the criminal element which in the circumstances described had things all their own way. The criminal element, though numerous, were in the minority. They had the advantage of being thoroughly organized and armed, and skillfully led by a man name "Soapy" Smith, who was the uncrowned King of Skagway. He was not a constitutional monarch, but his word was all the law there was."

Whenever travelers to the interior undertook to redress outrages they were frustrated by legally constituted authorities backed by soldiers. In making a complaint the miner whose investment in an outfit scattered along the trail was given to understand he must go before a commissioner, make his complaint and give bonds or be jailed for his appearance months hence at a trial held hundreds of miles away. Redress meant ruin and he bore his wrongs in preference. Officials were executing the laws but the laws were inapplicable to the conditions. Criminals flocked to a country that thus became an elysian for grafters. It was this climate that Jefferson Randolph Smith had stepped into when he arrived in Skagway.

"This puzzling, sentimental, and even foppish man, for all his moral callouses, was not without a following of friends and admirers, men and women outside of his criminal ring. There were two Smiths, doing good deeds and bad. His tremendous conceit would not permit him to be less than dictorial. He lived for homage. In return, if there was a church to be built or a fire hose to be purchased, Smith would do it. He supported widows and their children, especially those who were left destitute by sudden acts of violence. He always sent out $20 bills to the needy for Christmas, an idea which struck him in Denver and which continued self-righteously throughout his short life. He was happy to administer justice at all times whether it was over a runaway girl or a waterfront strike. His decision closed the altercation.

"The wealth that came to Smith disappeared almost as quickly as it was gained. He simply gave it away. He was known as a soft touch, providing the hard-luck story had a sincere, if familiar, ring to it. He gave shelter to any number of penniless Klondikers and kept them from starving to death that first winter in Skagway. That he might have been responsible for their condition was beside the point.

"He fed stray dogs. Hundreds of them had been kidnaped along the West Coast and brought north. When it was discovered that they were practically useless for hauling freight, they were dumped on the streets of Skagway. Jeff started an 'Adapt A Dog' movement and managed to find homes for most of them. He kept six himself and fed any strays that had been overlooked in the drive, with butcher shops and the like told to feed them and he would pick up the tab.

"Few argued with Smith. Rather there was generous adulation given to the swashbucking frontiersman. For here was a man of depth and insight, well versed in the foibles of human nature. He was a man of perception and he was in an occupation that brought him into contact with all strata of society. In Smith the town had found a man who could influence and control the recalcitrant mischief-makers. It was toward this conclusion that Soapy had so artfully directed his efforts. And he had won fairly, according to his standards.

"In the absence of constituted legal authority Jeff Smith, himself, became the law. He was the final court of appeal, public safety rested in his hands. From his headquarters and on the street he exuded grace as he arbitrate disputes, dispensed largess and administered justice while his henchmen stripped the gullible."

Soapy was responsible for many civic activities one of which proved extremely popular for families, in as much as it provided entertainment, other than the type available in the gambling halls, saloons and dance halls, during the daytime and on Sundays — not that the day of the week made much difference.

This was a baseball team which he managed and coached as well as provide uniforms and equipment. The team accepted a challenged from their rivals in Dyea, according to a story in the Skagway newspapers.

"Dyea, Alaska, June 9, 1898 - To Jeff Smith, manager of the would-be Skagway Base Ball Club. Recognizing the fact that you have some would-be baseball players, we hereby challenge you to play us three games for money, beans, or marbles, the first game to be played at our grand city on Sunday, June 19, at our Baseball Park.
Signed, Dyea Baseball Club, Champions of the World.

History - and local news coverage being such as it was in those days - fails to reveal if the series was ever completed. It is certain, however, that if baseball talent was available in Skagway and Jeff fielded a team which did itself proud, it more than likely came home with the money — rather than the beans or marbles.

CHAPTER 24
FOURTH OF JULY

Jeff was a soft spoken Georgian who for a few flamboyant months could say of Skagway, "I'm boss of this merry-go-round." He came to Skagway with the intent of becoming boss, an ambition he quickly achieved.

For a bad man, Smith was pretty good. Soapy was essentially an organizer. He was a self-appointed city manager who specialized in making over communities where the citizenry was distracted by silver and gold. In return for the right to fleece visitors, Soapy did his best to promote civic improvement and discourage gunplay. He was a sincere advocate of passive resistance, particularly on the part of his victims. He hated a complainer. All he asked was that a customer in his saloon take his losing quietly. He exercised no little ingenuity in making his mulching painless.

So important did Smith become in the community that it gave the public little shock when the Skagway newspaper referred to him as the Honorable Jefferson Randolph Smith when he was thanked by the War Department for a patriotic offer to equip and train a company for the military during the Spanish-American War.

The Fourth of July was a day patriotic Jeff Smith could not resist without a celebration and a parade. As a result Skagway saw one even bigger and better than that of his Skagway Guards a couple of months earlier.

The Skagway streets were gaily decorated with colors for the Fourth - miles of bunting and acres of flags. There were rockets and fire crackers, the popping of six-guns and exploding of dynamite in the hills, blaring bands and marching men all provided by Soapy..

Carriages were sent to homes through the area, courtesy of Jeff Smith, so that the women did not have to walk through muddy streets and sidewalks to the downtown area. Each was presented with a bouquet or corsage. Children munched on free candy and peanuts, the male adults had their bellies warmed by free whiskey, all provided by Smith.

Although organizing behind the scenes and providing most of the funds, Soapy did not head any of the committees and was not Grand Marshal of the parade as related in many instances. He did head the Fourth Division, the Skagway Guards and their band.

The Grand Marshal was G.W. Everett, a Skagway wholesale commission merchandiser. The Committee Chairman was W.F. Lokowitz, superintendent of the Burkhard Brewery. Frank Reid had been invited to take part in the program, but refused out of jealousy when he learned of Soapy's participation.

The winning float in the Fourth of July parade featured six-year old Frank Clancy, son of Soapy's partner, dressed as Uncle Sam, and a caged eagle which became a visitor attraction in Soapy's Parlors. Clifford Collection.

The four division marshals were S. L. Lovell, a prominent Skagway attorney; Charles Hansen, well known local business man; Frank H. Whiting, Superintendent of the White Pass & Yukon Route railroad substituting for WP&YR president S.H. Graves; and Jeff Smith. The latter's division consisted of the First Regiment of the Alaska Milita, a patriotic float (which won first prize) and the J.H. Brooks pack train.

The winning float was a four-wheeled flatbed wagon with a recently captured Bald Eagle in a cage, red, white and blue bunting, six American flags and John Clancy's six-year old son Frank dressed as Uncle Sam. The eagle latter was put on display as a visitor attraction in the yard back of Soapy's Parlor.

Territorial Governor John G. Brady from Sitka was in the reviewing stand as a guest of Jeff Smith and addressed the citizens of Skagway following the parade.

Smith sat next to Gov. Brady on the speakers platform and according to associates, was offered a high ranking position in Territorial Government by the Governor. Acceptance possibly could have saved his life.

In addition to the colorful parade, the Skagway's Fourth of July celebration included foot races and other activities which for the most part were held on Holly Street, in front of Soapy's Parlors, the small building on the right. - Yukon Archives.

The rest of the afternoon saw athletic events including a baseball game between Dyea and the Soapy's Skagway team, a series of foot races featuring a 100-yard dash for "fat men" with a keg of beer to the winner. Numerous Indian canoe races were held on the waters of Lynn Canal. Other events included horse races, a tug-of-war, grease pole climbing and much more.

The evening was devoted to concerts and plays and a gala fireworks display. One of the saloons featured the notorious Little Egypt who had become a star attraction on Seattle's raunchy waterfront. Such was Skagway's first Fourth of July celebration.

Although they were utterly ignored, the Territory of Alaska had very rigid federal laws prohibiting the sale of alcoholic beverages of any kind. As a result, all hard liquor shipped into Alaska ports was bonded for delivery to Canada. Yet, by some "mysterious" process, only barrels of water crossed the border at White Pass.

This situation probably had more to do with Soap's demise at the hands of Frank Reid than any single event.

The evening of July 7, the same day that John D. Stewart arrived in Skagway with his poke of gold, a load of choice liquor came in on one of the steamers and was picked up late that night by one of the the distributors of spirits for the area. As was the practice in those days,

This photo, taken in Smith's saloon by T.E. Peiser late in the evening, shows Soapy Smith with some of his close associates. Nate Pollock is the bartender. Next to him is "Rev." John Bowers, Smith's partner John Clancy, Soapy, Al White known as the Sheeney Kid and Harry Bronson, alias Red. - Clifford Collection.

arrangements had been made for the customs officers to be looking the other way when the load left the dock.

Soapy's men, having received a tip on the shipment, posed as customs officers and laid in wait for the load as it came off the dock. They hijacked the liquor. As the shipment had been brought ashore illegally in the first place there was no resistance from the teamster when they stopped the wagon and let him "escape" rather than face "arrest."

The load was taken to the back of Jeff's Place where it was unloaded and the team turned loose.

Soapy spent most of the next day making rounds of the saloons to which his followers had sold the haul. Although he rarely drank, Smith was more than willing to "buy a round for the boys," at each of the saloons and partook freely in the celebrations, accounting for his intoxicated condition later in the day.

His brain was afire with liquor — which was not his style. He was in the exact mood for trouble.

BOARDING PASS

Instant Travel™

Alaska Airlines | Horizon Air

Seat	Flight	From	To	Boards	Gate	Date
16F	82	H ANCHORAGE	SEATTLE TACOMA	242P	B8	AUG22

CHECK ID

ALBRIGHT/DAVIDMR

4LN/ANC

Earn Bonus Miles with 24-Hour Web Check-In at alaskaair.com!

alaska-air.com

partners with *horizonair.com*

Earn Free Travel Faster!

CHAPTER 25
ENTER JOHN D.STEWART

As July 7 dawned, a lone prospector, John D. Stewart, was making his way down the White Pass trail from Atlin, where he had been fairly successful in his gold mining efforts.

Stewart was toting a buckskin bag of gold nuggets worth roughly $2,700, according to those he proudly showed it to on stops along the trail as well as when he arrived in Skagway.

Stewart was an experienced miner who had prospected with success in the Pacific Northwest and the Yukon prior to the Klondike rush. A powerful man, about six foot two inches tall, he was married and resided in Nanaino, B.C. but had returned to the northland during the Klondike rush. Instead of the Yukon, however, he worked on his cousin's extensive holdings at Atlin and was returning home with his poke of gold when he stopped over in Skagway.

It was in a Skagway hotel the day before his boat was to sail that Stewart met and chatted with two strangers according to his daughter, Hazel Stewart Clark, when interviewed some time later. This was not unusual as everyone was friendly. Stewart told them about the gold he was taking out and the strangers suggested that he was taking a big chance carrying so much gold with him when so many men had been robbed. They suggested that he put the poke in the hotel vault, which he did.

The next morning when he went to get his poke from the hotel safe he was told that it was not there, and that no one there had ever seen him before.

Other versions as to the disappearance of the gold included the report in the Skagway News extra dated July 8.

"The cause which led up to the trouble (referring to Smith's and Reid's scuffle) had its origin in the morning shortly before 10 o'clock when J.D. Stewart, a young man just out from Dawson, was robbed of a sack containing from 12 to 15 pounds of gold. There are conflicting stories as to how the robbery was committed. The accepted version being that Stewart desired to sell his gold and that Rev. Bowers, a well known member of Jeff Smith's gang, represented to Stewart that he was here for the purpose of buying gold for some big assaying company below. The unsuspecting stranger accompanied Bowers to a point in the rear of Soapy's place on Holly Avenue near the Mondamin Hotel where it is alleged that two of Bowers' pals were waiting when the three men overpowered Stewart, wrestled the sack of gold containing $2,700, from his hands and disappeared from sight around adjoining

Prospector John D. Stewart (second from right) posed with his fellow prospectors at Atlin prior to heading down the trail to Skagway. - Clifford Collection.

buildings leaving the returned Klondiker as poor as when he started for the land of gold and hardships nearly a year ago."

The Daily Alaskan dated July 9, reported:

"The trouble that ended in the shooting affray, began yesterday at noon. J.D. Stewart, one of the returning Klondikers, was rolled and robbed of a sack containing about $3,000 in nuggets and dust. Mr. Stewart said that he had gone into Smith's place looking for a companion. He walked out in the back yard with the bag swung on his shoulder and was looking at the eagle. He found out there three men who, from the description given of them afterwards, are supposed to have been Joe Bowers, an old man named Tripp, and another man called Dick. The three men began to play monte, Stewart says, and finally began to scuffle. He took no part whatever in the game. In a moment or two he found them brushing up against him, and before he knew it two of the men grabbed him and the third snatched the bag from him and ran. The two men held him until the third had gone away. Then they too ran in a different direction. Tripp is said to be the one who got the bag."

Another version was printed in the Rocky Mountain News in January 1900, related by Dr. J.S. McCue, a friend of Smith's from his Colorado days. Dr. McCue stated he was with Soapy in a Skagway hotel just prior to the shooting and that Smith related the following story.

"The man (J.D. Stewart) who lost the money lost it because he thought he had a sure thing and was going to clean out the members of Soapy's gang he was playing with. After watching a three-card monte game in Soapy's saloon they finally 'let' him into the game. They let the sucker win a few dollars and then his 'friend' who had taken no part in the game showed him a way he could beat the dealer. He said he would call the attention of the dealer to some object nearby and when he was looking at it the sucker could turn the top card and knowing what it was, could bet on it for a sure thing.

"This tickled the sucker and the trick was tried. It worked to perfection and he saw a way to clean out the house as he supposed. He asked them to wait a minute while he went over to the hotel to get his pile which was about $2600. He got it and came back and started in the game again.

"They let the sucker win at it again and then the friend proposed that they beat the dealer by the same method that had worked before. The sucker agreed and while the friend called attention to a caged eagle

The last photo of Soapy Smith while he was alive taken by Rev. John A. Sinclair on Broadway at 9 a.m. on July 7, 1898 as Smith was on his way to his office on Holly St. He was fatally wounded late the next day. - Clifford Collection.

the victim turned the card and saw that it was an ace. He then bet the whole pile on it. The long and short of it was that when the card was turned it was a jack and the sucker saw his pile go into the pocket of the dealer.

"Soapy reported that after Stewart raised such a howl - stronger than anyone had raised before - he was in favor of giving back the money. Reverend Bowers and the others, however, would not have it and they deposited it in The First Bank of Skagway until they could divide it."

Another theory is that it was a well known fact that although Smith was the so-called "King of the Underworld" in Skagway, there were other gangs operating and not paying tribute to him. All were jealous of his success and position in the community. The possibility that one of the reasons that Smith did not return Stewart's gold was that a group other than Soapy's had taken the poke and he was not about to pay that amount when his followers were not responsible for the crime. Instead, in asking extensions in the time of when he would "return" the gold was that he had his followers trying to locate those responsible. Smith's past history had been that whenever such an occasion arose with the authorities involving his men he had been more than willing to make restitution.

John D. Stewart openly bragged of his "poke of (photo 3 inchs gold" to one and all in Skagway and then seemed caption baffled when it "mysteriously" disappeared. Such 1 inch) was the key to the shoot out on Skagway's Juneau Wharf which took the lives of Jefferson Randolph "Soapy" Smith and Frank H. Reid. - Clifford Collection.

When Stewart finally realized that he had been taken, no matter what the story, he went to the Marshal Taylor and detailed his loss of the gold, but with little success. When asked if he could identify the culprits, Stewart stated that he could not, and hence was told by the marshal there was little that could be done.

Not satisfied, Stewart went to some local merchants telling his tale of woe. Some were interested in that Stewart had ordered a couple of suits of cloths from them, and with the loss of his gold, he could not pay. They felt that this was money out of their own pockets.

Frank Reid got wind of the situation. Some suggested that Reid himself had set up the whole affair in order to get a chance to renew the feud between the two committees and to get at Soapy.

There were those who also contented that Reid's and Stewart's paths had crossed and that Reid talked Stewart into setting up Soapy and his followers in order that the Vigilante's could get rid of him one way or another.

Such was the start of the most interesting and controversial days in the colorful histor of Skagway.

CHAPTER 26
SHOOTOUT ON THE WATERFRONT

No matter what, Stewart's actions resulted in a meeting of the Merchant's Committee composed of some of the most respected businessmen in the community who had no personal axes to grind. Their thoughts being to do what was best for Skagway in the long term. Some of the group were respected members of the Vigilantes and represented that group. Seventeen members of the committee met following Stewart's complaints and named Samuel H. Graves, president of the White Pass and Yukon Route railroad, chairman. They then adjourned to allow Judge Charles A. Schlbrede, who had been called over from Dyea, and others time to work out a satisfactory arrangement for the return of the gold. They agreed to meet again at 11 p.m. to decide upon what action to take.

In the meantime, Frank Reid and others, unknown to the committee chairman or other members, decided to call upon Soapy, demanding that the gold be returned - as was often the case when a rumpus was in the making. They set a 4 p.m. deadline which ruffled Smith considerable.

Commissioner (Judge) C.A. Schlbrede was one of many who tried unsuccessfully to straighten things out following John D. Stewart's loss of his prized poke of gold. - Clifford Collection.

Meanwhile Judge Schlbrede attempted to settle matters. His task, however, had been made difficult in Reid demanding that Smith return Stewart's gold by 4 p.m. Judge Schlbrede called Smith to his hotel room and ordered him to return the gold by 6 p.m., stating that warrants would be issued for all concerned, including Smith, should he not comply. Soapy was most unhappy and returned to Jeff's Place.

When Smith made no attempt to meet either the 4 or 6 p.m. deadlines for returning the gold some of the Vigilantes, despite the original meeting's adjournment until 11 p.m., concluded that things were not moving as fast as they would like. The Committee called a secret meeting in the Sylvester warehouse for 8 o'clock in the evening without notifying Graves. So many people showed up that after electing Thomas Whitten of the Golden North Hotel, chairman, they adjourned as the Sylvester warehouse proved to be too small.

The meeting reconvened on Juneau wharf where there was a large warehouse at the far end without notifying Graves.

Whitten's first action was to post guards at the shore end of the long wharf to keep any strangers — especially Soapy's followers who had gained entrance to the early session — from taking part. Reid was the only one of the four who was armed, having borrowed a Colt police revolver from a friend earlier in the day although it was not his custom to carry a weapon.

As far as the Committee was concerned, it was rather strange that a meeting was being held without Samuel Graves, who only a few hours previous had been named chairman and had set a meeting for 11 p.m. that evening. Graves, however, a recent arrival, was not one of the original Committee of 101 or Vigilantes composed mostly of those who had jumped Capt. Moore's homestead.

According Graves' report to superiors in London - to which he added local color and excitement so that the British investors would not be disappointed in reading of the great frontier - the dock meeting had been called by others without his being notified. This brought about Graves' conjecture that another gang had taken over or the committee was bent on destroying Smith without him having the opportunity to defend himself.

When Smith learned of the second meeting he left his saloon for the dock shortly before 9 p.m. He had received a note from Billy Saportas, who had covered the previous meetings as a reporter, stating, "The crowd is angry. If you want to do anything do it quick." Confident that once again he could bluff his way out of trouble as he had in the past, Smith left the saloon with his trusty Winchester over his arm, expressing his confidence.

"I'll drive the bastards into the bay."

He moved west along Holly St. to State, which ran parallel to Broadway, and then turned south toward the waterfront, muttering that he would "teach these damn sons of bitches a lesson."

Behind him at a respectful distance a crowd of curious people, including some of his cohorts, followed. Smith swung his rifle off his shoulder and waved it like a fly-swatter.

"Chase yourselves home to bed," he shouted to the few bystanders along the route.

The crowd hung back, but did not disperse. A few of his followers swung in behind them, at a distance of some 25 or more feet.

Others, sensing danger, had already fled to the hills.

One of the last to talk with Soapy on his way to the dock was John Clancy, Smith's erstwhile saloon partner, who was out for a walk with his wife and six-year old son. As Smith passed them Clancy tried to dissuade him from going to the wharf, but Smith was in no mood to chatter.

Clancy was unable to convince Soapy to change his mind, and Smith said, "Johnny, you better leave me alone" and he urged them to return home.

"All right," Clancy replied in disgust. "If you want to get killed, go ahead." As they stepped aside to let Soapy pass, Mrs. Clancy began to cry.

The Skagway News reported what followed:

"The Vigilantes had posted a committee of four, Frank H. Reid, Jesse Murphy, J.M. Tanner and Mr. Landers to guard the approach to the dock in order that no objectionable character might be admitted to disturb the deliberations of the meeting.

"It was while this committee of four was stationed at the head of the dock that Jeff Smith appeared, carrying a Winchester rifle in his hands. He walked straight up to Reid and with an oath and apparent

Skagway's Juneau Wharf at the left, where Frank Reid and Soapy Smith met their doom while the Vigilantes were holding a meeting in the warehouse on the end of the dock. The shore end is at Runnels Street (now State Street). - Clifford Collection.

bluff, asked what he was doing there and at the same time striking at him with the barrel of the gun. Reid grabbed the gun in his left hand as it descended, pushing it down towards the ground, drawing his revolver with his right hand at the same time. When the point of the rifle was close against Reid's right groin Smith pulled the trigger. The ball passed clear through and came out through the lower part of the right hip. At the same time Reid fired two or three shots in rapid succession, one of which pierced Smith's heart, another striking one of his legs. Smith also fired a second shot striking Reid in the leg. Both men fell at about the same time. Soapy Smith stone dead and chief engineer Reid dangerously, perhaps mortally, wounded."

In describing the action Graves, who was with Frank H. Whiting,the railroad's division superintendent, stated.

"I saw Soapy go to Reid and make a bluff to hit him over the head with the barrel of his rifle. Reid put up one hand and protected his head by catching the barrel. Soapy, failing to shake off Reid's hold, jerked back the rifle suddenly which brought the muzzle against Reid's stomach. Reid still held Soapy's rifle with one hand as before but put the other slowly in his coat pocket, and without taking it out again commenced to shoot his revolver. Soapy at the same instant began to pump shots from his Winchester into Reid's stomach.

"It would be impossible to say which fired first, the shots were absolutely simultaneous. Each fired four shots, though one of Reid's first shots had gone clean through Soapy's heart.

"It was not murder so much as a sort of spontaneous killing. Neither had any intention of killing a moment before, but they must have seen death in each other's eyes at the last moment and both fired together. They fell together in a confused heap on the planking of the wharf. Soapy of course stone dead and Reid dying. It all happened in an instant."

Another dependable witnesses was Robert E.(Bobby) Sheldon Jr., a 14-year old newsboy at the time, who oftimes delivered Seattle newspapers to Soapy.

Shelton related his version of the shootout to Soapy's grandson, Randolph "Randy" J. Smith in Seattle in 1973 when Randy was attending an auction of some of Soapy's possession belonging to Harriet Pullen.

Sheldon stated he was about 100 feet away when Smith and Reid met. He stated that he could see a heated argument going on between the two, and that Soapy pointed his Winchester at Reid, who grabbed the barrel with his left hand and reached for his revolred with the right.

Soapy was the first to fire his weapon, Sheldon reported. Despite being hit, Reid was able to fire three times with each bullet leaving its mark on Soapy's body. Both collapsed on the dock.

Sheldon stated that it was a quiet evening and that there were not a great number of people about. As far as the report that Smith possibly was shot from ambush, Sheldon said that he did not hear any other shots and that if one had been fired he was certain that he would have heard it.

Sheldon stated a former White Pass employee, Willie Flynn, related the story that Smith was shot from ambush to tourist, but was unable to substantiate the report.

Another witness was Calvin H. Barkdall, a prospector and pack train operator and a friend of Reid's.

Barkdall noted that Reid and a little Irishman had taken their post as outside guards at the approach to the dock.

"All was going well when we looked up the street and noticed Soapy Smith coming around the corner, a Model 86 Winchester in his hands, ready for action. The muzzle was pointed low, his left hand on the forearm, his right hand on the trigger. Frank Reid had a police revolver.

"Reid stepped out in front of him and said, 'Halt, Smith. Where are you going?'

"At that Soapy raised his rifle, said, 'Get out of my way you son of a ....' and slashed at Reid's head.

"Reid jumped back, drew his revolver. I heard it snap — a miss fire.

"As Soapy brought his rifle down from striking at Reid, he fired and struck Reid in the right groin. Reid's first shot struck Soapy in the heart. The second his stomach. Murphy then grabbed Soapy's gun.

"Both men fell within a couple of feet of each other. Smith had been killed instantly. Reid was mortally wounded."

At the sound of shots, those Vigilantes meeting in the warehouse came running out, some armed and others just shouting. Any thoughts of the half dozen or so of Smith's followers to contend with them disappeared as they took off in all directions.

The Vigilantes went to a nearby cabin and brought out a cot which was used as a stretcher to carry the severely wounded Reid to his home nearby and then to the office of Dr. J.J. Moore. Other physicians including Drs. C.W. Cornelius and Bryant arrived, and it was determined that Reid should be moved to the Bishop Rowe Hospital, where it was discovered that his wounds were more serious than first believed. Smith had been a large contributor to the hospital as Bishop Rowe raised funds for its construction.

Smith's body was left lying on the dock until the wee small hours of the morning when one of the town's females, believed to have been Harriet Pullen, had it removed to the Peoples Undertaking Parlors.

CHAPTER 27
WHO SHOT SOAPY?

Within a few minutes of the shooting Skagway was in an uproar. Josiah M. Tanner, a former sheriff in Pierce County, Wash., who had been sworn in by Judge Schlbrede to replace Deputy Marshal Sylvester S. Taylor, as deputy marshal, ran up Broadway calling his townsmen to arms.

In less than half an hour after the shooting more than 200 citizens were organized into a company. They searched every house or building suspected of harboring one of Smith's followers and guards were put on the wharfs, along the bay and the hillsides. The WP&YR, when notified of the occurrence, set guards north of the city and on the bridges in an effort to round up the remnants of Smith's group. Some had made their way to the hills, or escaped towards Dyea.

Many of the posse members did not know who they were looking for and often anyone who could not explain their mode of life was locked up in the city jail until a hearing could be held.

One who escaped to the hills, but returned when hunger pangs got the best of him and found no trouble in sneaking back into town was Old Man Tripp. He was captured in the Pack Train Inn as he was

An angry crowd outside of Skagway's City Hall/Jail threatening to lynch Smith's followers after the shootout on the Skagway waterfront. The timely arrival of army troops from Dyea prevented bloodshed. Clifford Collection.

Newspaper headlines from around the country tell the story of Soapy Smith's demise.

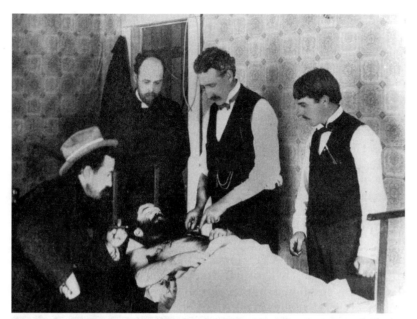

Dr. F.B. Whiting examines the fatal bullet removed from Soapy's body during the autopsy while Calvin H. Barkdull (seated), Rev. John A. Sinclair and Dr. C.W. Cornelius served as witnesses. - Clifford Collection.

having an early morning steak breakfast. He was allowed to finish his meal and was put under heavy guard on the upper floor of the Burkhard Hotel. Tripp had been hiding out with Bowers, Slim Jim and Wilder who were captured later when Tanner sent a group of 30 armed men to seek them out. Late in the evening, after the trio was booked into the Burkhard, crowds began to gather, many with ropes, demanding that the prisoners be turned over to them.

An earlier telephone call had alerted troops in Dyea under Capt. Richard T. Yeatman. They arrived just as some of the Vigilante leaders attempted to break down the door to the upstairs room where the four were being held.

Slim Jim Foster made a desperate leap out of the rear window hitting the ground running. Scores aimed their rifles and fired, but Foster escaped untouched. He was captured at Bond and States Streets. A rope was being drawn around his neck as the troops arrived. Foster was returned to his prison room unharmed.

The autopsy on Smith was performed July 9 in the Peoples Undertaking Parlors by Drs. F.B. Whiting and C.W. Cornelius. They reported that two slugs entered his body. One hit him in the thigh and the other went into the right side of the chest, crossing the body to the left and going through the heart.

Two questions which were not published arose in the report. One was to the effect that it was impossible while the two men were facing each other for a slug from Reid's weapon, held in his right hand, to enter Smith's body at the angle it did on the right side and pass through the body and heart. The other was that the calibre of the fatal slug did not match that of Reid's borrowed Colt. One bullet was a 38 caliber, the other was not listed.

These questions added fuel to the reports that it was impossible for Reid to have been the person who fatally wounded Smith.

An inquest on Smith was opened a few hours later at the undertaking rooms. Judge Schlbrede presided as coroner and F.F. Clark, A. Louseneister, G. Chealander, C. Neice, A.E. Cleveland and W.O. Henn were sworn in as jurors. The two doctors testified that they had conducted a post-mortem and found that death had been instantaneous. A great mass of evidence was introduced and so carefully was it sifted that except for a brief luncheon recess the hearing continued uninterruptedly until late in the afternoon.

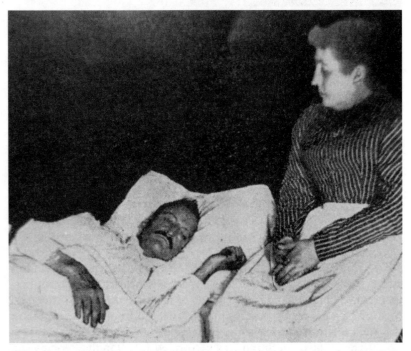

Photograph of Frank H. Reid taken by Rev. John A. Sinclair in the Bishop Rowe hospital during his last hours. - Clifford Collection.

112

Bishop Rowe Hospital where Frank Reid died on July 20, 1897, 12 days after the shootout on the Skagway's Juneau Wharf. - Clifford Collection.

Several witnesses claimed that the fatal shot had been fired by Jessie Murphy.

Some witnesses were certain that it was not Reid who fired the fatal shot. Murphy, a popular figure in town, was named instead despite the fact that he was unarmed when the shooting started.

Others stated that Murphy grabbed Soapy's rifle after he fell. There was no evidence that the rifle was fired after it left Soapy's grasp or while in Murphy's posesesion.

Some contend Murphy grabbed Reid's firearm and shot Soapy although none of the witnesses reported he firing the weapon. Another report had Si Tanner coming up to the prone Reid, asked him where his gun was. Reid rolled off the gun and Tanner picked it up.

So confusing were reports on the shooting between Smith and Reid that a well recognized Skagway resident, Frank J. Clancy, who as a youngster saw the shooting in a different light. He described his version in the Alaska Sportsman of October 1955 as follows:

"- - Soapy kept coming and stepped over the barrier. Reid pulled the trigger on his rifle. It clicked on a bad cartridge. Then Reid pulled the trigger again, the rifle roared almost simultaneous with Soapy's 45. Reid's bullet hit Soapy in the chest and Soapy's bullet hit the big City Engineer. Both were mortally wounded. —"

The article goes on and points out that Clancy's father was the executor of Smith's estate which included the Colt .45 revolver which

113

Which one killed Soapy Smith? Official credit is given Frank Reid (left), although many felt that it was impossible for a bullet from Reid's revolver to enter Smith's body at the angle it did. Also the calibre of the bullet did not match those in Reid's borrowed revolver. Turner Jackson (right), Smith's bodyguard, had his pistol in hand pointed in the direction of the two combatants at the time the shots were fired. It's calibre was not checked, nor was it examined as to whether it had been fired. It was believe that Jackson aimed at Reid in an attempt to save Smith, but hit Jeff instead. - Clifford Collection.

remained in his father's possession until his death in 1945 when it passed on to the author. It is a Colt Frontier Six Shooter patented Sept. 10, 1871. The number stamped on the butt and frame is 143179."

Most witnesses had it the other way - that Reid had the revolver and Smith the rifle.

During the confusion it was very possible that Turner Jackson, one of Smith's followers who also served as a body guard for Soapy, could have fired the fatal shot while aiming at Reid. Such was noted later at the trial of Jackson in Sitka where he was charged with assault with a deadly weapon against Josiah M. Tanner at the time of the Reid shooting. He was sentenced to 10 years at McNeil Island penitentury in Washington State.

Regardless the jury awarded the honor to Frank Reid.

"We the jurors called to inquire into the cause of the death of Jefferson Randolph Smith, after having each and all of us examined the body of said Smith, and having heard the evidence of Dr. Cornelius and Dr. Whiting upon the medical examination of said body, and also evidence of witnesses who were present at the death of said Smith, which took place on Juneau Wharf, City of Skagway, District of Alaska, U.S.A. between the hours of nine and ten p.m., on July 8, 1898, hereby find:

"That said Smith came to his death by reason of a pistol wound piercing the heart.

"That said wound was the result of a pistol shot fired by one Frank H. Reid, who now lies in the Bishop Rowe Hospital of Skagway, dangerously wounded from shots received at the hands of the deceased, the said Smith.

"That such shooting on the part of the said Reid was in self-defense, and in the opinion of this jury entirely justifiable."

The support for Murphy was an honest opinion of many, apparently because he was a popular figure in town, and they were certain that it was not Reid who fired the shot or shots.

This gives credence to someone else being the one who fired the fatal shot, as Murphy was unarmed at the time.

Smith, at the time, was in front of several of his followers. He went by Tanner and Murphy and approached Reid. At the same time, Jackson drew his revolver and pointed it at Tanner. After Smith was shot, Jackson reholstered his revolver, and with the others of Smith's associates, beat a hasty retreat from the wharf.

Jackson was arrested by Tanner some 26 hours after the shooting while sleeping in the Astoria Hotel. Tanner took Jackson's loaded revolver from him at the time.

During the trial in Sitka some weeks later, when asked about the gun and cartridges, Tanner, who had handled guns for more than 30 years and was considered knowledgeable although not an expert on guns stated, "I can't always tell as to the freshness (of the cartridges), but I examined the gun the next morning, and I considered them fresh cartridges." The question as to whether the gun had recently been fired and reloaded was not brought up. During the trial the jury fired the weapon successfully.

It was shown in court that during the shooting and confusion "it was impossible to exclude the fact as to what occurred at the time of the assault."

It was possible that Jackson, who was some distance away, fired in an attempt to shoot Reid, missed and hit Soapy instead. So confusing were things during the shooting that one of the guards (Landis) judged Jackson was about five feet from Tanner, another thought it was 10 to 15 feet and Tanner himself judged it was 20 feet or more. Soapy and Reid were even a greater distance away.

The action, for the most part, took place on a section of the wharf which was about 16 feet wide and 60 feet in length. Jackson was at one of the shore side corners with his back to those citizens on shore. They were unable to see what he did with his pistol.

The confusion also could account for the question of the varying number of shots fired with testimony of witnesses varying from four to eight being heard during the fracas. None other than Jackson were named as having drawn a firearm at the time.

This single action 45-caliber Colt revolver with a 7 1/2 inch barrel is, as far as can be determined, the weapon that killed Soapy Smith. Manufactured in 1875 by the Colt Firearms Co. it bears the number 20105 and has three notches. It belongs to Dick Ryman of Glenwood Spring, Colo. and was obtained by the Rymans from Billy Meservy, alias Billy Bard, a family relative who was in Skagway and Nome during the gold rush. - Dick Ryman photo.

It was said that Reid gave "his life for the honor of Skagway." Perhaps Jackson should have beeng so honored instead of being sentenced to 10 years at McNeil Island Penitentiary in Washington State. Recently brought to light is information on the weapon credited with the killing of Soapy Smith in Skagway. It is in the possession of Dick Ryman of Glenwood Springs, Colo. Ryman received the weapon in a gun and Indian artifacts collection left by his grandfather, Charles W. Ryman, formerly of Lincoln Neb. The weapon was sent to the senior Ryman close to 100 years ago by his brother-in-law. Information on the weapon at the time was that it was "the weapon that killed Soapy Smith."

The elder Ryman's brother-in-law Billy Meservy was in Skagway and later Nome during the gold rush years. He had committed a crime earlier and escaped to Alaska. He assumed the name "Billy Bard". As such he could have been one of Soapy's followers and associated with Turner Jackson.

It is known that Reid carried a "borrowed" weapon at the time of the shooting but it did not match the fatal bullet. Meservy's single action Colt-45 revolver with a 7 1/2-inch barrel was manufactured by the Colt Firearms Co. in 1875 and was number 20106. It was marked with three notches.

Such, could have been carried by Jackson and obtained by Meservy following the trial in Sitka.

CHAPTER 28
FUNERALS SERVICES

Rev. John A. Sinclair preached the sermon at Smith's funeral on Monday, July 11 after both the Baptists and Methodist ministers refused to do so. Others had indicated that his body should be dumped into the waters of the harbor. The Rev. Sinclair felt otherwise.

Smith's body was open for viewing shortly before the services. Rev. Sinclair reported that there were seven men and one woman at the funeralThe text from Proverbs 13:15 was "Good understanding getting favor but the way of the transgressor is hard."

The coffin was taken to the cemetery in an express wagon with the undertaker and driver on the wagon seat. It was preceded by a hack in which rode Mr. Butler, a prominent member of the Vigilante Committee, three lawyers who had done work for Soapy, a late partner of the deceased and Rev. Sinclair. The body was buried six feet outside of the cemetery boundary so as not to desecrate the cemetery grounds.

Frank H. Reid's funeral on July 22, 1898, was the greatest in the history of Skagway. Services were held in Skagway's first church, at the near right. - Clifford Collection.

Reverend Sinclair was given Soapy's small Derringer in lieu of a fee and later he received a heart-warming letter from Soapy's sister in Temple, Texas thanking him for giving her brother a Christian burial.

Prior to the funeral two Victoria men, C.O. Von and Herbert Savage along with a Victoria doctor, had attempted unsuccessful to purchase or otherwise obtain Soapy's body. They planned to put it on display in the major cities of the West, especially in Colorado, Idaho and Montana where Smith was well known and not at all unpopular.

The Rev. Sinclair had spent considerable time with Reid in the hospital and was surprised with the greeting he received from Reid following his officiating at Soapy's funeral.

He felt that he had possibly offended Reid in so doing and mentioned such to him.

"Not a bit of it," Reid replied. "You did perfectly right and the fools who said he should be thrown in a hole like a dog are savages! No matter how many kinds of a devil a man has been, his corpse should have a Christian burial. It's only savages who dishonor their dead."

Reid's wounds, at first thought to be not too serious, became worse infection set in. He passed away in the Bishop Rowe Hospital on July 20, 12 days after the shooting.

He was found to have been hit by a Winchester 45.80 caliber rifle bullet, the ball entering two inches above the groin on the right making its exit an inch to the right of the point of the spinal column. The ball made a comminuted fracture of the pelvic bone and several fragments were removed by Dr. F.B. Whiting at the time of the examination.

Reid's body lay in state in a flag draped coffin in the Union Church from 10 a.m. to 1 p.m. on July 22 and was followed by a

Frank Reid's body guarded by members of the Alaska Guards as it is on display in the church prior to funeral services.- Clifford Collection.

The original wooden marker on Jefferson Randolph "Soapy" Smith grave a few months after his burial and the same marker some years later after being removed and displayed in Seattle. At present the marker is part of the Jeff Smith Collection in California. - Clifford Collection and H. Clifford Photo.

funeral which according to the Daily Alaskan, "Skagway's first public funeral was the greatest popular demonstration that Alaska has ever known." The Rev. Dr. Wooden conducted the services reading the ritual for the dead of the Episcopal Church. The Rev. Sinclair delivered an elegant tribute in the memory of Skagway's hero.

A large marble marker was placed over the grave with the inscription "He gave his life for the honor of Skagway."

CHAPTER 29
THE AFTERMATH

After spending a few days in jail following the roundup some of the so-called members of Soapy's gang, for which no charges had been filed, began to talk about "their rights." according to S.H. Graves who apparently back as chairman of the Merchants Committee. He also reported that some of the prisoner's money was used illegally to repay the money missing from Steward's poke. He stated that they could give the Vigilantes a good deal of trouble if they dared in as much as they were being held against their will and there was no shadow of law to warrant their imprisonment. Even less was the taking of money found on them and using it to pay for the stolen gold dust, for a fund to pay the expenses of legal prosecutions against them and pay the cost of "deporting" the others.

Graves reported that one of the prisoners who referred to his "rights" was taken to a window of the room in the Burkhard Hotel where he was being held. He could see the unruly mob outside. At the same time Graves stated to him that, "Yes, we have no authority for holding you against your will. If you say the word, we will turn you loose into the mob this minute."

Needless to say, the prisoner changed his mind.

The committee went further, and demanded that each prisoner sign a paper, requesting that the committee hold and protect him until he could be handed over to lawful authorities, and in consideration for this protection the committee was given all the money he had on him for the use of the committee.

This allowed the committee to get out of a false position, provided for the stolen gold and to carry on prosecution for which they had legal evidence against.

Some of the gang were marched to the wharf, lined up and photographed before being shipped out aboard the Tartar. All signed papers (under duress) declaring that they left of their own free will. The Committee of 101 paid their transportation costs - with their own money.

Nine of those shipped out, including W.F. Saportas, reporter for New York World; Nate Pollock, bartender at Soapy's Place, who gave the name of W.W. Jennings; C.S. Hussey; Bradley O'Brien; Chas. Bromley (Bromberg); J. A. Swain; J. Leary (Cleary); Frank Brown (alias Blue Jay) and Henry Smith were sent through bond to Victoria and on to Seattle. Dr. J. Allen Hornsby, editor of the Daily Alaskan and friendly to Smith as well being a member of the city council, school board and leader of the Commercial Club, was "advised" to go with the group.

Soapy Smith's followers photographed prior to their enforced departure from Skagway. Nate Pollock, Jeff's Parlors bartender is fifth from the left and William Sarpolis to his left. Also identified is Charles Bromberg (Bromley) at the far right. - Clifford Collection.

When the group arrived in Seattle, they were warned by Chief of Police Reed, that they would be picked up and jailed should they remain in the area. Only one, however, was arrested. He was Charles Brom, a youngster of 21 years who was known as a right bower man. He was held for safe keeping, photographed and then shipped out of town.

Later six men, possibly another gang were deported on the ship Tees. They were: Wm. Tener, Billy O'Donnell, Jim (John) Hawkins, Mike J.Torpy (Talpy), Bert Markinson (Madison) and F.J. Dugronder alias "Doc". Vie Torpy (Mike's wife) refused to go and was jailed under bond.

Among those sent to Sitka for trial were: W.E. "Slim Jim" Foster alias Deep Sea Carter, Van B. Tripplett alias "Old Man" Tripp (age 74) and (Reverend) John Bowers, said to be the three identified by Stewart as those who robbed him. Each was found guilty and sentenced to one year in jail in Sitka.

George Wilder, received 7 years, Turner Jackson 10 years, and John Clear, fined $5,000 all for assault with a dangerous weapon. Harry L. Bronson (alias Red) was charged with larceny but it was "found not a true bill" and was released.

Others included Charles Butler inciting riot, S.S. Taylor (former deputy marshal) dereliction of duty, Al L. White alias Sheeney Kid larceny and being armed with a dangerous weapon. Arrested but not charged were H. Ranshman alias Tommy, William Fielding and James H. Neiman. Sixteen others were released because of lack of evidence and were advised to leave Skagway.

Four of Smith's close followers, "Slim Jim" Foster, "Rev" John Bowers, Turner Jackson and Van B. Tripplet alias "Old Man" Tripp, photographed aboard ship on their way to Sitka for trial. - Clifford Collection

A total of 26 had been arrested. The total was a small figure compared with reports and stories to the effect that Soapy's gang numbered 200 to 300.

After the hearings and deportations the entire "city council" with the exception of Chairman Sperry, resigned or had been deported. The citizens of Skagway decided to hold an election, still without a vestige of legal warrant. A Mayor and City Council were elected, and a Chief of Police appointed. This body carried on the city government until Congress finally extended the provisions of the Homestead Act to cover Alaska, bringing the Territory under U.S. laws for the first time.

The Skagway News carried a report in the July 15 issue to the effect that a large portion of the 123 1/3 ounces with a value of about $2,100 had been found in a trunk in a shack back of Soapy's saloon.

The paper stated that the gold was returned to the original owner who beamed and smiled broadly on receiving it. The story suggested "that when Stewart reached Nanaimo B.C., where he had a wife, it is hoped that his lady will take him across her knee and administer her slipper in good style. It will learn him to postpone looking at eagles in the future until after he disposes of his wealth."

No matter what the story, his Skagway experience brought to an end the adventuresome spirit of Stewart. Upon returning home with

Monument erected by the citizens of Skagway at the grave of Frank H. Reid (left) and simple marker on the grave of Jefferson Randolph Smith located a few feet outside the original border of the cemetery. Soapy's grave is probably Skagway's most visited historic attraction. H. Clifford photos.

his gold, he settled down, worked for a mining company in Nanamio until 1912. He became interested in mine safety and rescue work and was appointed superintendent and instructor at the Government Mine Rescue Station. He retired at age 65 and died in 1930 at 84.

Smith's probate under direction of his partner Clancy, showed little in the way of assets in Skagway other than half ownership in the Jeff's Parlors. .

Some historians reported that Soapy buried part of his ill-gotten gains, $40,000 to $50,000 or more in money and dust, in the mountains above Capt. Moore's original dock. Such has never been verified and many old timers reported that they had never heard of such.

Smith's widow with their oldest son arrived in Skagway a short time after his death. After a short visit they returned to St. Louis with Capt. Johnny O'Brien paying for the transportation as a small token for Smith having saved his life some years earlier.

Smith's grave was marked with a plain board which later was taken as a souvenir and split in half by some baseball players who came up from Seattle to play for the Skagway team originated by Soapy. The marker was said to have been displayed at a University of Washington fraternity house for many years. It is now in possession of the

125

family. Over the years the grave fell into disrepair. Later Harriet Pullen received $50 from Thomas Kearny of St Paul an old friend of Smiths, with instructions to see that the grave was properly cared for. This continued annually for many years during which several markers were destroyed by souvenir seekers and replaced.

News of the death of Smith was carried worldwide, with many papers and magazine carrying lengthy stories of his life.

Soapy's death however, did not immediately put an end crime in Skagway. Wilson Mizner returning from Dawson reported that in his opinion things were much worse in Skagway in as much crime was in the hands of "amateurs." A couple of years later one of the banks was bombed in an attempted robbery but the would be robber blew himself up in the blast.

Wilson Mizner later became one of the most notable gamblers on trans-Atlantic ships, and an associate of society gambler Arnold Rothstein when the latter won $800,000 betting on a single horse race. This also got him barred for life from the New York tracks. For a short time Mizner was married to Myra Adelaide Yerkes, the "second richest woman in the world." He also became a stage actor and playwright, art dealer, manager of Stanley Ketchel the great middleweight boxing champion, promoter of the $30,000,000 Boca Ratan real estate deal, a Hollywood script writer and director. He was also a partner with Herb Somborn, former husband of Gloria Swanson, in the Hollywood Brown Derby and led the "parade" of entertainment greats to Palm Springs.

While a film writer, Mizner's great ambition was to do a picture on Soapy. A Hollywood magnate became enthusiastic and commissioned him to write a script. Mizner leaped at the project with one of his rare bursts of energy, but the picture was never made. The studio wanted the Skagway belles to be Sutton Place debutantes with Antone coiffures and Paris boudoir armament. Mizner held out for two-fisted, slammerkins with top knots and red flannel underwear.

Later Los Angeles police Capt. Lefty James, an authority on gaming in talking of Mizner, said "Nobody in America is qualified even to discuss the subject in that man's presence." Such was the teachings of Soapy Smith.

Wilson passed away in Hollywood from a heart attack in March 1933 at 58 years of age.

He is also remembered for his many quotes such as "The only sure thing about luck is that it will change," and described Hollywood as "the land where nobody noes."

Despite Bobby Sheldon's youth, he remained in Skagway as his father had passed away. Later he worked for a harbor boat operator. He also owned the first automobile in Alaska, building it himself from

InstantTravel ™

Alaska Airlines / Horizon Air

BOARDING PASS

CHECK ID

Seat	Flight	From	To	Boards	Gate	Date
16E	82	H ANCHORAGE	SEATTLE TACOMA	242P	B8	AUG22

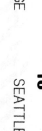

ALBRIGHT/ELAINEMS

alaskaair.com -- Earn Bonus Miles and Travel Free Faster!

4LN/ANC

boat and buggy parts, without ever having seen one. He later did construction work, became a state representative, Mt. McKinley National Park concessionaire, Fairbanks postmaster, and founder and operator of the Fairbanks-Valdez Auto Stage Line using Model T Fords for transportation. Sheldon eventually moved to Seattle, but returned to Pioneer Home in Fairbanks where he died in December 1982.

The fact that the First Bank of Skagway had initially occupied the Soapy Smith's Parlors building may have in part accounted for the report, never confirmed, that money taken from Stewart was stashed in the bank's vault. When questioned about the money one of Smith's cohorts stated that it had been deposited in the bank. The charge was denied by bank officials, but the story affected the bank's credit and it went into the hands of a receiver on July 17, 1898 with liabilities of $16,000 and assets, such as they were, listed at $18,000.

Mrs. Pullen, died in Skagway in 1947 at age 87. She possibly was closer to Smith than many people were aware of as many of his personal possessions came into her hands and her booklet of the life story of Jefferson Randolph Smith closed with a graceful finale.

"Thus ends the story of Jefferson Randolph Smith, a story of character, of a man, taking the wrong trail and mushing to an ignoble

end, dieing as he had lived, defying law and order. There are many "Soapy" Smiths in the world today, no better or worse, only lacking the opportunity of becoming famous as he did.

A Flake of Snow makes the Glacier,
A drop of water the Sea,
A little thought for good or bad,
Makes or mars our Eternity.

The End.

Harriet Pullen in one of her favorite "Native American" outfits. - Clifford Collection.

BIBLIOGRAPHY

BOOKS

ADNEY, EDWIN TAPPAN. - The Klondike Stampede of 1897/1898. Ye Gallion Press. Fairfied 1968.

ANDREWS, CLARENCE L. - Wrangell and the Gold of the Cassiar. Luke Tinker Commercial Printers. Seattle. 1937. The Story of Alaska. Caxton Printers Ltd. Caldwell. 1938.

ANZER, RICHARD C. (Dixie). - Klondike Gold Rush. Pageant Press. New York. 1959.

BANCROFT, CAROLINE. - Denver's Lively Past. Johnson Publishing Co. Boulder. 1952
"Machless Mine & Lusty Leadville. Johnson Printing, Boulder. 1960.

BANKSON, RUSSELL R. - The Klondike Nugget. Caxton Printers Inc. Caldwell. 1935

BEATIE, KIM. - Brother, Here's A Man. MacMillan Co. New York. 1940.

BECKER, ETHEL ANDERSON. - Klondike '98. Binsford & Mort. Portland. 1949.

BEER, THOMAS - The Mauve Decade. Alfred A. Knopf. New York 1926.

BERTON, LAURA BEATRICE. - I Married the Klondike. Little, Brown & Co.Boston 1954.

BERTON. PIERRE. - Klondike Stampede. Alfred A. Knopf. New York. 1956.

BILSLAND, W.W. - Atlin 1898-1910. Atlin Centennial Committee. 1971.

BLACK, MARTHA LOUISE. - My Seventy Years. Thomas Nelson & Sons. New York. 1939.

BLAIR, EDWIN and CHURCHILL, E. RICHARD. - Everybody Came to Leadville.B and B Printers and Lithographers. Gunnison. 1972.

BURTON, PIERRE. - Klondike Fever. Alfred A. Knopf. New York. 1958.

CHASE, WILL. - The Sourdough Pot. Burton Publishing. Kansas City. 1943.

CLARK, HENRY W. - History of Alaska. MacMillan Co. New York. 1930

CLARRIDGE, DAVID and JULIE. - A Ton of Gold. Private Publisher. Seattle. 1972.

CLIFFORD, HOWARD. - Skagway Story. Alaska Northwest Publishing (AlaskaBooks). Anchorage. 1975
Rails North. Superior Publishing. Seattle. 1981.
Doing the White Pass. Sourdough Enterprises. Seattle. 1983.

COHEN, STAN. - The Streets Were Paved With Gold. Pictorial Historic Publishing Missoula. 1977'
Gold Rush Gateway. Pictorial Historic Publishing Co. Missoula. 1986.

COOPER, MICHAEL. - Klondike Fever. Clarion Books. New York. 1989.

COLLIER, WILLIAM ROSS & WESTRATE, EDWIN VICTOR - The Reign of Soapy Smith. Doubleday, Doran & Co. Garden City. 1935.

DALBY, MILTON A. - Dynamite Johnny O'Brien. Lowman & Hanford. Seattle. 1933

DeARMENT, ROBERT K. - Bat Masterson. University of Oklahoma Press. Norman. 1979.

DeARMOND, R.N. - 'Stroller' White: Tales of a Klondike Newsman. Mitchell Press, Vancouver B.C. 1969.

DENNISON, MERRILL. - Klondike Mike. William Morrow & Co. New York. 1933.

DORSET, PHYLLIS FLANDERS. - Colorado's Gold and Silver Rushes. Barnes & Noble Books. New York. 1994.

ELMAN, ROBERT - Badmen of the West. Castle Books. Secaucas, N.J. 1874.

FEITZ, LELAND. - Soapy Smith's Creede. Little London Press. Colorado Springs. 1973. A Quick History of Creede. Golden Bell Press. Denver. 1969.

FRIESEN, RICHARD. - The Chilkoot Pass and the Great Gold Rush of 1898. Ministry of Supply & Service. Ottawa. 1981.

GRAVES S.H. - On the White Pass Payroll. R.R. Donnelley & Sons. Chicago. 1908.

HARRIS, A.S. - Alaska and the Klondike Gold Fields. Monroe Book Co. Chicago.1897.

HELLER, HERBERT L. - Sourdough Sagas. Ballentine Books, New York. 1967.

HENDRICKS, GEORGE. - The Bad Man of The West. Naylor Co. Sam Antonio 1942.

HERRON, EDWARD. - Dynamite Johnny O'Brien. Julian Messner Inc. New York. 1962.

HINES, JACK. - Minstreal of The Yukon. Greenburg. New York. 1948.

HULLEY, CLARENCE C. - Alaska 1741-1953. Binford & Mort, Portland. 1953.

HUNT, INEZ & DRAPER, WANETTA W. - To Colorado's Restless Ghosts. Sage Books.

HUNT WILLIAM R. - North of 53. Macmillan Publishing Co. Inc. New York. 1972
Distant Justice. University of Oklahoma Press. Norman. 1987.

INGERSOLL, ERNEST. - Gold Fields of the Klondike. Mr. Paperback. Langley, B.C. 1897. (Reprint 1981). Original (1897).

ITJEN, MARTIN. - Story of The Skagway Streetcar. Skagway, 1938.

JENKINS, THOMAS. - The Man of Alaska. Morhouse-Corman Co. New York. 1943.

JOHNSTON, ALVA. - The Legendary Mizners. Farmer, Straus and Young.New York. 1953.

JONES, NARD. - Seattle. Doubleday & Co. Garden City. 1972.

KOBRE, SIDNEY. - The Yellow Press and Gilded Age Journalism. Florida State University.

LUCIA, ELLIS. - Klondike Kate. Hasting House Publishing. New York. 1962.

MARTIN, CY. - Gold Rush Narrow Gauge. Trans Angelo Books. Los Angeles. 1969.

McKEOWN, MARTHA. - The Trail Led North. Macmillan Co. New York. 1948.

McLOUGHLIN, DENNIS. - An Encyclopedia of the Old West. Barnes & Noble. New York. 199

MILLER, MIKE. - Soapy. Alaska Books. Juneau. 1970.

MINTER, ROY. - The White Pass Gateway to the Klondike. University of Alaska Press. Fairbanks. 1989.

MIZNER, ADDISON. - The Many Mizners. Sears Publishing Co. New York. 1932.

MOORE, BERNARD J. - Skagway In Days Primeval. Vantage Press. New York. 1968.

MORGAN, MURRAY. - Skid Road. Viking Press. New York. 1951. One Man's Gold Rush. University of Washington Press. Seattle. 1967.

MORTINSON, ELLA LUNG. - Black Sand and Gold. Metropolitan Press. Portland. 1969.   Trail to the North Star. Binsford & Mort. Portland 1969.

MUMBY, NOLIE. - Creede. Artcraft Books. Denver. 1949.

NASH, JAY ROBERT. - Bloodletters and Badmen. M. Evans & Co. New York. 1973

NEWELL, GORDON & SHERWOOD, DON. - Totem Tales of Old Seattle. Superior Publishing Co. Seattle. 1956.

O'CONNOR, RICHARD. - Highjinks on the Klondike. Bobbs-Merrill Co. New York. 1954.

PARKHILL, FORBES. - The Wildest of the West. Henry Holt and Co. New York. 1951.

PETERSON, ART & WILLIAMS, D. SCOTT. - Murder, Madness and Mystery. Castle Peak Editions. Williams, Ore. 1991.

POYNTER, MARGARET. - Gold Rush. Atheneum. New York. 1979.

PULLEN, HARRIET S. - Soapy Smith, Bandit of Skagway. (Reprint) Sourdough Enterprises. Seattle.1973.

PRINGLE, GEORGE. C.F. - Tillicoms of the Trail. McClelland & Stewart. Toronto. 1922.

ROBERTSON, FRANK G. & HARRIS, KAY. - Soapy Smith, King of Frontier Con Men. Hasting House. New York. 1961.

SATTERFIELD, ARCHIE. - Chilkoot Pass-Then and Now. Alaska Northwest Publishing. Anchorage. 1973.

SAMUELS, CHARLES. - The Magnificent Rube. McGraw-Hill Book Co. New York . 1957.

SAWATSKY, DON, - Ghost Town Trails of The Yukon. Stagecoach Publishing Co. Langley B.C. 1975.

SHEA & PATTEN.- The Soapy Smith Tragedy. Daily Alaska Print, Skagway 1907. (Reprint) Sourdough Enterprises, Seattle. 1972.

SHIELS, ARCHIE W. - Sewards Icebox. Union Printing. Bellingham 1932.

SINCLAIR, JAMES M. - MISSION: KLONDIKE. Mitchell Press, Ltd. Vancouver. 1978.

STANTON, JAMES B. - Ho For the Klondike. Handcock House Publishers, Saanichton. 1974.

SPEIDEL, WILLIAM C. - Sons of the Profits. Nettle Creek Publishing. Seattle. 1967.

STUMER, HAROLD MERRITT. - This Was Klondike Fever. Superior Publishing. 1978.

SULLIVAN, EDWARD DEAN. - The Fabulous Wilson Mizner. The Henkle Co. New York. 1935.

THOMAS, LOWELL JR. - The Trail of '98. Duell, Sloan and Pearce. New York. 1962.

THOMPSON, DISESUALD. - Historic Round Rock. Round Rock, Tex.

WATT, BOB & NANCY. - Skagway. 1969.

WHITING, F.B. MD - Peacock Publishing Co. Seattle. 1933. .

WICKERSHAM, JAMES. - Old Yukon - Tales, Trails and Trials.
Washington Law Book Co. Washington D.C. 1938.

WINSLOW, KATHRYN. - Big Pan-Out. W.W. Norton. New York.
1951.

WOODS, HENRY F. - Gods Loaded Dice. Caxton Printers.
Caldwell. 1048.
Klondike. The Chicago Record Book for Gold Seekers.
Chicago Record. 1897.

PERIODICALS

Alaska Life. Where in Hell is Soapy? June 1944.
Little Known Facts About the Life and Death
of Soapy Smith. April 1942.
Klondike or Bust. Aug. 1946.
Captain Billy, April 1944
Alaska Magazine. Gamblin' Man. May 1967
Alaska Sportsman. Gold Rush Bad Town. April 1939
The Hero of Skagway. Vol. VII. No. 8. Aug 1941
Soapy Smith. Vol VII. No 5. May 1942
Man of Skagway. Silver Jubilee Edition. 1943
The Real Soapy Smith.Vol. XIII, No. 11. Nov1947
Long Voyage to Fortune. Vol. XXI. Aug. 1955
I Was Just a Kid. Vol. XXX. No. 10. October 1955
A Man of Honor. March 1958.
This Month in History. Nov. 1963
First Christmas in Skaguay. December 1969
This Month in History. Vol.. XXXV, No. 6. June 1969
Alaska -Yukon Magazine. Correspondence of a Crook. Dec. 1907
Vol. IV. No.4. Jan. 1908. Vol. IV No. 5
American West. Vol. II, No 2. Spring 1965.
B.C. Outdoors. Captain W. Moore - Frontiersman. Nov. - Dec. 1972,
Vol. 27. No. 6. Jan. - Feb. 1972, Vol. 28. No. 1. Mar. - Apr.
1972, Vol. 28, No. 2. May - Jun. 1972, Vol. 28, No. 3. Jly. -
Aug. 1972. Vol. 28, No. 4.
Decision. The Gambler and The Lady. July 1965.